This book is dedicated
To all my children
Who always need to lovingly remember?

Call Your Mother!

Part One

It's a Really Safe Place as Long As There's Not a Murder

Hadley: It's safe here, BUT – one night someone slipped into my apartment and stole my thighs and gave me these awful ones with veins and dark spots and flab. A genuine thigh-theft caper.

Robbie: The same gang came into my place and stole my stomach and butt! They gave me somebody else's saggy buns and a stomach that is much bigger than when I went to bed.

Mary Rose: I woke up one morning and my boobs were gone. Then I saw they had slipped into my armpits. Of course later, someone actually did steal one of my boobs and not only that, he charged me for doing it.

They looked at **Marge Aaron**, retired homicide detective. It took a minute then she said, "My face. Some thief stole my face and left me with this wrinkled, saggy, eyebrowless visage that has droopy lids and lips. This is a serious crime spree!"

A Dead Body on the First Page

Ralph "Percolator" Rasmussen lay face down, spread-eagled, on the dining room floor of Meadow Lakes Retirement Community. The back of his head was smashed in, his throat had been cut, there was a nylon cord around his neck, a bullet hole in his jacket and a knife in his back.

"Are we sure he's dead?" Mary Rose McGill asked.

"If he isn't, he'd better have damn good insurance," Wiley Vondra said.

Robinson Leary put her hands on her hips. "This is ridiculous! No publisher will print a book with a dead body on the first page. Now I suppose we'll have to put up with some weird vampire in a creepy funeral home."

Hadley Joy Morris-Whitfield and Mary Rose McGill looked at each other.

"Uh-oh," they said together.

And so our story begins...

Minnie Mouse with A Bad Hangover

The body had been removed. Mary Rose, Hadley and Robbie were sipping decaf at Table 12 by the window in the large dining room. The entire section where Perky Rasmussen's body had lain was cordoned off with yellow police tape. From where they sat, the girls could see two men in dark suits and three uniformed officers sitting at a table next to the tape and talking earnestly to John, the Meadow Lakes manager.

"He was a mean, mean man," Hadley said of the victim.

"Perky never had a kind word for anybody," Robbie added. "But he didn't deserve to die, at least not like that."

"He was *murdered*," Mary Rose added. Her eyes were bright with excitement. She loved everything to do with mystery, action, crime and spies. "Murdered. Offed. Bumped off. Hit. Done in." She took a breath. "Assassinated. Knocked Off. Iced. Liquidated. Whacked."

"In other words, he's dead." Robbie said.

"We should catch the killer." Mary Rose put her elbows on the table and leaned toward them. "If Calamity were here, she'd already be on it."

Calamity Doodles had been a BOOB Girl: A Burned Out Old Broad, two years ago. Her mother had been head of a circus Wild West show and her father had been the head clown. Calamity had led them to rob a grave and destroy a gangster's mansion, which meant she had obviously turned out to be a lot of fun.

Now there were only three at Table 12. Shortly after her husband died, Mary Rose McGill, the lover of mysteries and adventure, had arrived at Meadow Lakes with fourteen housedresses, two sweaters, two plain coats and two pairs of ugly, clunky shoes. That same husband had a massive stroke while attending mass and died a few days later. Thanks to the love and friendship that happens only between women, Mary Rose had lost sixty pounds, had her hair dyed blonde by the best stylist in Omaha, dressed in bright clothes and wore classy, red-rimmed glasses. She patted Robinson Leary's hand and nodded as if to affirm the fact that they needed to get right on catching the killer.

"Perky's tongue was so sharp he could have cut his own throat," Robbie said. "But that doesn't explain the noose, the bullet hole, the knife or getting in the way of a blunt instrument to the back of his head. Some wiseass would probably say it's the most thorough case of suicide they'd ever seen."

Dr. Robinson Leary was a retired English Professor from Creighton University in downtown Omaha. She was half black, half Cajun, making her skin the color of a rich mocha coffee or a creamy latte. Her husband, who was the love of her life, had been a very long-time Multiple Sclerosis patient. He had been wheelchair bound and when he died in his sleep, Robbie showered, dressed, went to their bank and cleaned out their safety deposit box before she called anyone. When a teller had greeted her and asked where her professor husband was, Robbie had simply said, "He's still in bed." She never did find out if the rumors she had heard about safety deposit boxes being sealed after a death were true or not. She didn't need to.

Hadley Joy Morris-Whitfield reached over and patted both her friend's hands. She smiled.

"Remember how Calamity told Percolator Rasmussen how she could tell how old he was by looking at his private parts? She got him to drop his pants and his drawers."

"He had on shorts with turtles on them, and one was right in the front," Mary Rose laughed a soft, tinkly laugh.

Hadley went on, "He jumped around with his pants around his ankles three times, just like Calamity told him to, then we said, 'You're eight-four years old!' And when he asked how we could tell his age just by looking at his junk, we said. . . ," She looked at the other two.

"We were at your birthday party last week," they all said together and they laughed so loud that the two serious suits sitting with John near where the body had been gave them a stern look. There was no one else in the dining room and sound really carried when the place was empty.

Mary Rose leaned back in her chair then got up. "I have to pee. Remember how our mothers used to want us to always have clean underwear with us in case we were in an accident? Well now I carry clean underwear with me in case I *have* an accident." She headed toward the ladies room near the dining room entrance.

Hadley looked after her friend scurrying toward the bathroom and smiled. "As Wanda Sykes says, we used to stick clean underwear in our purses in case we got lucky. Now we stick clean underwear in our purses in case we *sneeze*. And now we're such techies that Mary Rose has a PoopLog app on her smart phone."

Hadley's husband had died in a plane crash. She was tall, stately and wealthy. It was Hadley's spacious apartment on the nice third floor of Meadow Lakes that welcomed them when they planned things, watched movies and entertained. Her husband had never been the most loyal, but he was the most loving and now her son, who was on his fourth marriage, reminded Hadley more and more of his father.

Mary Rose hurried out of the ladies room and scurried across the floor toward Table 12. Just as she reached them she stopped short. "OMG!" She pointed out the big window that looked over the Meadow Lakes parking lot.

Robbie and Hadley turned in their chairs. Robbie smiled and said, "OMG. Mary Rose is texting her grandchildren way too much." Then she leaned forward and stared.

Pulling into the parking space between the girls' gigantic black Hummer and Frieda Grossemouth's fin-tailed pink Cadillac was the gaudiest Smart Car they had ever seen. It was black. Painted all over it were big, bright pink polka dots. Huge white plastic eye lashes loomed unblinking over the headlights.

Mary Rose sat down. They were all turned toward the three cars lined up and facing them, the little Smart Car looking dwarfed between the Cadillac and Hummer.

"That smart car looks like Minnie Mouse with a bad hangover," Hadley said.

"I think it's rather sweet," Mary Rose said with her most motherly smile. "It looks like the Hummer and Caddy had a baby."

"A really ugly baby," Robbie said. "I'm anxious to see the idiot who drives something like that."

They could see the idiot's two basketball-player sized feet reaching for the pavement underneath the driver's side door. Both feet were encased in plain black walking shoes. Then a red cane tip joined the feet. Finally, feet and cane were followed by a woman-mountain of a female.

Taller than Hadley, who was five-ten and hadn't really shrunk much, this lady was massive, impassive, impressive and tough; not fat, just big-boned, big-limbed; BIG. She wore a black pants suit with a red scarf looped around her neck, a neck so short and stubby it was almost non-existent. Her hair was gun-metal grey with short spikes all over her head in what was actually an attractive style for her. She had black-rimmed glasses; a black brief case that hung on a long strap slung over one shoulder and she carried the red cane over one arm like a purse.

"Bling," Mary Rose said, pointing to the cane.

The red walking stick was a work of art. It was covered with big, different colored fake jewels; red, green, purple, diamond, yellow and white. They could see a huge sparkly ring on the hand nearest the cane. Their heads all turned together as the big woman sauntered down the sidewalk outside the window, then turned and walked through the double doors and into the dining room.

Hadley realized they were all holding their breath and blew hers out. She heard Robbie and Mary Rose exhale together in one quick *whoosh*.

The big lady walked directly toward Table 12, never taking her eyes off the three women seated there. She came to a stop behind the empty chair. She stared at each woman separately for a second. Hadley, Robbie and Mary Rose lifted their heads to look up at her. She had on bright red lipstick and her eyes behind her black-rimmed glasses looked determined and in total control. She plopped her cane and briefcase down on the table and dug into the pocket of her black pants. She took a second to look at each of them again, then tossed a silver badge in a black case onto the table beside the cane.

All three BOOB Girls continued to stare at her with their mouths open.

"I'm Marge Aaron, retired homicide detective. I'm on this case, and this is my station now.

You're welcome to stay if you don't ask too many questions and you don't try to take over my business." And with that she walked, caneless and unlimping over to the two men in black who were seated with John, the manager.

All three men stood up. For a minute Hadley thought they were actually going to bow as if Marge Aaron was some sort of royalty.

"That was weird and rude." Hadley was frowning and watching the big woman. "Who does she think she is, anyway?"

"She thinks she's Marge Aaron, retired homicide detective." Robbie was grinning and looking after the big woman. Then she leaned toward Hadley, putting both of her forearms on the table. "*Marge Aaron.* Say it fast and it sounds like 'margarine.'"

Hadley grinned back and put both her arms on the table as well. "Then she'd *butter be good!*"

Mary Rose mimicked their arms on the table positions and leaned forward to whisper. "I wonder if she spreads easily."

"Mary Rose McGill!" The other two said together. They laughed, but this time they made sure it was a quiet laugh.

What and McGill

Marge Aaron's big body hid most of the action at the table across the dining room where she had settled in with the three men. The girls could see they were talking seriously and rapidly.

"Filling her in on details," Mary Rose said knowingly. "Bringing her into the loop. Giving her the scoop, the low down. Updating the case. Bringing her on board."

"Sounds more like newspaper talk than crime talk," Robbie said.

In a few minutes, big Marge stood up, turned and headed back toward Table 12. The two suits followed on her heels and John, Meadow Lakes manager, made a fast exit through the dining room doors toward the safety of his office.

"I want you to meet What and McGill," Marge said, pointing to the two men. "They're the lead detectives on this case. They'll be working with me."

"What?" Robbie said.

"These are Detectives What and McGill," Marge repeated.

"No – his name is What?" Robbie said, a smile crinkling her cheeks.

"What."

"Who, What?"

"Oh," Marge said, "It's *Wadsworth*. What. And yes, his last name is What."

Hadley and Robbie both did eye rolls.

Mary Rose actually raised her hand. "And *I'm* McGill."

Silence.

"I mean I'm a McGill, too," Mary Rose insisted. "Mary Rose McGill." She looked at the other McGill invading her territory at Table 12.

McGill the detective looked at Mary Rose, smiled slowly and said nothing . . . slowly.

Slowly was his thing. Detective McGill bore all the presence of a man looking for Second Street in a one street town. Finally, he stopped rotating his head. Finding his focus with his one good eye, he spoke . . . slowly.

"Spose we're related? You know . . . I mean, family. I've got McGills on both sides of my family. So much so I am my own cousin – a double cousin. I could hold my own reunion once a year."

No one smiled. He seemed serious. While Detective What was nearly bald, McGill had a wild, uncontrolled mass of white hair. It looked as if a seagull had landed on his head and died there.

"Ugly enough to choke a buzzard," Hadley whispered to Robbie out of the corner of her mouth. Robbie nodded and did another eye roll.

"Well, there you are. I can see the possibilities," Mary Rose nodded, moved her hands back and forth, then got up from her chair and took a step back. She was standing next to Marge Aaron, as if she was trying to hide in the big woman's shadow.

"Don't underestimate him," said What." We need McGill. He's got a good eye."

Only one, Hadley thought, and she watched as Detective What leaned around in front of his partner, looked toward McGill's good eye and said. "Tell us again what happened to the victim."

Mary Rose became excited and spoke up before the other McGill could open his mouth. "The back of his head was smashed in, his throat had been cut, there was a nylon cord around his neck, a bullet hole in his jacket and a knife in his back." She said it all in one breath.

Marge Aaron spoke up. "So with all that, which is it? Is the killer vindictive....or just indecisive?"

"Either way," What said, "the killer was thorough, and we even have some questions about a possible chest wound as well."

At that point, Marge Aaron took over and did a very strange thing. She pointed her red cane at Hadley and looked directly into Hadley's eyes.

"Hadley Joy Morris-Whitfield. If Jesus is the son of God, Morris-Whitfield here is His favorite niece. More money than God, she masterminded a successful grave robbery and in an earlier book she located Just Plain Bill Porter, the gangster."

"Actually...." Hadley started to say, but Marge moved on.

She pointed the cane at Robbie, "Dr. Robinson Leary, also known as 'The Professor,' successfully blew up Porter's mansion, closed down a sleazy porn shop early in her career and brought down the infamous J. Frederick Sapp."

"That wasn't me, "Robbie said with an innocent tone. "Calamity Doodles and Maggie Patten did those things...." Robbie looked confused, and Dr. Robinson Leary didn't often get confused.

Marge turned the cane toward Mary Rose whose eyes were wide and her mouth open in a gigantic grin. "Mary Rose McGill," Marge continued. "Sweet Catholic girl. Found the hidden microchip in JPB Porter's mansion, was instrumental in taking down J. Frederick Sapp and she has minor bladder and bowel issues."

"That's me!" Mary Rose raised her hand again and bounced up and down once, then she sat back down in her chair.

Hadley and Robbie stared at Mary Rose, then both turned and stared at Marge.

"How do you know all this about us?" Hadley asked. She sounded amazed.

Marge Aaron shrugged. "I have a loving relationship with Google and I Tweet." Then she turned like an angry mother hen toward What and McGill. "Never underestimate a burned out old broad," she growled. Robbie wondered if they had been arguing when they were seated together at the other table. Marge sounded as if she was defending The BOOB Girls.

What ignored Marge Aaron and turned toward his partner. "And neither do we underestimate Detective McGill's good eye. It was McGill who saw the toenails."

Hadley stared at them. "Toenails?"

"Percolator dies on May 13th and that takes us to the toenails." Both detectives looked as if they belonged in an old **Pink Panther** movie that had ended up starring Peter Sellers as the Panther and Peter Falk with a walk-on role as Columbo.

"That day was St. Sevatus Feast Day. The patron Saint of foot problems. Percolator had ingrown toenails."

Now it was Hadley's turn to stand up. When she stood, her right knee creaked and popped. It was so loud Marge jumped a little and looked at Hadley. "He was stabbed. Shot. Strangled... and you wonder about ingrown toenails? What has that got to do with anything?" Hadley's voice kept on getting louder. This conversation was getting weirder and weirder.

"Sometimes we overlook the obvious," What explained. "The little thingies. A man is violently killed on St. Sevatus Day and he has feet issues. There is something there."

"Are you nuts?" Mary Rose's mouth was open in amazement. She stood up again, looking very short standing next to Marge and her cane.

"And did you actually say, 'thingies'?" Robbie asked. She stood as well and realized how really big Marge Aaron was.

What ignored Robbie and went straight to Mary Rose's, "Are you nuts?" question.

"No, I'm not Nutz," What said. "But do you know her?

"Who?"

"Lizzie B. Nutz."

"LIZZIE B. NUTZ???" the girls said together. They realized right away that Marge had spoken with them and was looking at the two detectives like they had worms.

"She does pedicures down at Toes in the Old Market." McGill spoke slowly. Marge was squinting at the two cops.

"There's more," What said, giving Marge a knowing look. "Every bit of blood was gone from that body. No blood even in the furthest extremity. And when it was over the body is laid out spread eagle in penance.....and then, whoever did all this trimmed his toenails and rubbed oil on his feet."

As if he had said something of great importance, What turned and started walking toward the door, looking for all get out like Peter Sellers thinking he had saved the day. McGill, who was looking more like Columbo, but without the brains, smiled at the girls, turned and followed What out the door. Slowly.

"They need to work on their people skills," Mary Rose McGill said as the two detectives went through the big double doors.

"They really do need to work on their communication," Robbie noted.

"They really do need to work on their manners," Hadley added.

Marge Aaron nodded. "They need to just plain work!"

Hadley, Robbie and Mary Rose looked at Marge, then at each other. They smiled. Hadley silently mouthed, "I like her." They all turned to Marge and grinned. There were four BOOB girls again at Table 12.

Marge Aaron: Love at First Bite

Things got back to normal quickly after What and McGill disappeared into Strange Detective Land. The girls discovered that Marge Aaron not only fit in as a fourth BOOB Girl, she was fun with a sense of humor as big as her ample behind. She had taken a small studio apartment on the third floor of Meadow Lakes, just down the hall from Hadley's big three-bedroom job.

It was a sunny morning with streaks of sunlight playing on the hardwood floor of Meadow Lakes dining room. The four girls were at Table 12 and Wiley Vondra had pulled up a chair close to Mary Rose.

Mary Rose McGill had a thing for Wiley Vondra and she knew Wiley Vondra had a thing for her; at least she was pretty sure he still did. Lately he'd been distant and wasn't appearing at her door as often. Right now though, she was so intent on reading a text from a granddaughter on her smart phone that she didn't notice his cup of coffee was untouched and while he was watching her, he wasn't interrupting with snickers or pats on her knee. He was just watching. Quiet.

Hadley looked at Wiley then at Mary Rose. "Wiley, you seem kind of down lately," she said.

Wiley shook his head. "No big deal."

Then he stood up, turned and walked toward the door leading to his wing at the retirement community. Mary Rose stood up with him but headed in the opposite direction toward the bathroom.

"What's with Wiley anyway?" Robbie asked.

"He's downright moody," Hadley added.

"I'd say let's ask his Honey Bunny when she gets back from the bathroom." Marge said. Just then the text alert on her smart phone buzzed the first two notes from "Law and Order."

She read the text, smiled and showed it to Robbie and Hadley. Mary Rose had texted, "LKI-HAGBM."

Robbie grinned and gave Marge's big arm a friendly slap. "Laxative Kicked In- Having A Good Bowel Movement."

"Mary Rose McGill texts. She has entered the 21st century," Marge said, taking a sip of her coffee. She drank regular, high-test coffee and ate whatever she wanted. She had several pantsuits, all of them either blue, black or grey, but today she was in a dark green jogging suit which meant she wasn't going to meet What and McGill or chase down any bad guys. She had settled into Meadow Lakes like a veteran. She was enjoying the company of the other women and leaving most days around three in the afternoon, always dressed in a pantsuit and carrying the briefcase and the red cane.

When anyone asked Marge Aaron how Perky's murder case was coming along, she would shrug her shoulders, roll her big eyes and then call What and McGill testosterone-depleted morons. While the girls seldom saw her black briefcase, the red cane was always leaning within reach, its jewels sparkling and blinging. Mary Rose hurried back from the ladies' room and sat down. Like Marge, she was dressed in a jogging suit, but hers was a soft pink which went well with her blonde hair. Hadley and Robbie were comfortable in jeans and HUSKER sweatshirts. On the outside of the big window Marge's polka dot Smart Car sat contentedly between the pink Caddy and black Hummer. It seemed to be watching its mistress like a loyal puppy, never blinking its big white plastic eyelashes.

Marge leaned forward, her elbows on the table and looked at Mary Rose. "What's going on with the Wiley Man, girlfriend. That cowboy is flatter than a cow pie on a rainy day."

Mary Rose shook her head. "I don't really know. He seems down, sad, morose, all the words I can think of that stand for 'not happy,' I asked him about it – more than once – and he just said he was bored. He needs some excitement and can't think of anything to do. He said he's too old for a midlife crisis so he must be having a 'Senior Setback'."

Hadley leaned toward Mary Rose and squinted at her. "Have you tickled his pickle?"

Robbie leaned in from her chair, "Have you diddled his doo-dad?"

Marge matched their lean-ins, "Have you noddled his noodle?"

Mary Rose put her forehead on the table and started to giggle. "I even told him he had a keener wiener." She looked up. "He didn't respond." And she laughed until tears came to her eyes.

But Wiley was, unfortunately forgotten, when Robbie announced she was going to research the evolution of the Vampire character in motion pictures and needed a movie marathon in Hadley's apartment for a day or two.

As soon as they left Table 12, Mary Rose McGill made tracks for the Meadow Lakes Library to get every current magazine available. When scary parts came in the movies Robbie researched, Mary Rose made even faster tracks to the bathroom where she read and looked at the pictures until it was safe to come out. Meg Noyes and Loretta Ripp were acting librarians and knew about the research marathons. They had watched the girls live through three days of Stephen King.

"What's Robbie up to now?" Meg asked.

"Vampires. Bloodsuckers. Neck Biters," Mary Rose sighed.

"I've got just what you want," Meg Noyes said. She was an attractive woman with sleek hair and a warm smile. She quickly rummaged around in a stack of magazines on her desk and pulled one out near the bottom. She handed it to Mary Rose.

"Bite Me?" Mary Rose said, holding it as if it might grow teeth right there in her hand.

"An award winner," Loretta Ripp called out from across the room. "It has some interviews with real vampires. We got it in a sample promotion."

Mary Rose shifted Bite Me to her left hand and made the sign of the cross with her right. "Jesus, Mary and Joseph," she whispered. "I'll take it for Robbie, but where are the *Ladies Home Journals* and *Good Housekeeping*?"

"I'm Going Out for A Bite to Drink."

Instead of dinner in the Meadow Lakes dining room, Hadley set in a good supply of microwave popcorn. Later, when it was popped, she would mix it with M&Ms, nuts and crunchy little goldfish crackers. Marge appeared at the door with three packs of diet soda and four bottles of cheap champagne. Smiling, she sat the sodas and champagne on the kitchen counter and leaned the red cane against a comfortable recliner, claiming it as her own.

Mary Rose handed **Bite Me** magazine to Robbie, who read the cover and raised her eyebrows. Then Mary Rose scurried into the bathroom and put her stack of safe magazines on the little table beside the tub. Robbie lined up the movies on the coffee table, then showed them to her friends as they worked in the kitchen.

"Okay, girls," she said, holding up one of the DVDs. "Here's the first one. It set the stage for nearly every vampire movie after it. It's a silent movie, **Nosferatu** from 1922 and modeled after Bram Stoker's famous, **Dracula**."

"If it doesn't have sound, maybe I can last all the way through it," Mary Rose said.

Robbie nodded, "Has music and that gets a little tad scary. But remember, Dracula actually became the most popular fictional movie character in film history. What's not to like about him?"

She picked up a second DVD. "Then we make a comparison with an old but more current film that has comedy implications for the toothy one; *Love At First Bite* with George Hamilton."

"I love George Hamilton!' Mary Rose grinned and squealed.

"It's funny, too," Robbie smiled. "When the girl says maybe they can have a quickie, Dracula says, (she added a silky accent), 'You are never a *queekie*. You are always a *longie*.' And when the bat flies through an apartment where the people are poor, they think he's a black chicken and try to catch him to eat him."

Marge turned from where she had fixed four sodas with ice and said, "And that's the movie where Dracula says, 'I'm going out for a bite to drink," and she grinned and showed what would have been fangs if she had any.

"Third movie," Robbie said, holding it up. "More serious and a real study in great literature. *Interview with the Vampire*, from the famous book by Ann Rice featuring the vampire, Lestat." She grinned at Mary Rose and tossed the DVD into her lap. "Brad Pitt, Tom Cruise and Antonio Banderas."

Mary Rose held the movie to her heart. "I may not go to the bathroom at all!"

"And the last is the newer *Twilight* trilogy, the neat, teen-girl, modern day vampire-werewolf combination by writer Stephanie Meyer.

Marge had passed out the sodas. "You have to love a Mormon girl who is into vampires and werewolves," she said.

"The werewolf is Jacob, the vampire is Edward and they are played by extremely cute young actors."

"With lots of muscle and tight buns," Hadley added "I read the books because my granddaughter was into them. I'd say they're Harry Potter for girls."

"Who doesn't want to be loved by two powerful men? And when those men are a werewolf and a vampire…bite me, claw me." Marge said, letting them know she had read the trilogy as well.

Robbie picked up another DVD. "And as we look at the evolution of the vampire in our culture, keep in mind that the vampire family in *Twilight* is 'vegetarian' who don't drink human blood. They're civic-minded citizens with an MD vampire father."

Hadley took off her shoes, crawled up on her couch and tucked her feet in behind Mary Rose whose shoes were beside the big soft footstool that held her stockinged feet.

Marge got the last bag of popcorn out of the microwave, mixed in the M&Ms, nuts and goldfish and divided it into the four bowls Hadley had set out. She was smiling and very much at home as she passed around the goodies. She and Robbie took the two recliners facing the television and both tossed their shoes into the middle of the floor.

Only Robbie had a notebook and pen on her lap. She pressed the remote and the strange music of a silent movie soundtrack filled the room. Hadley finished her bowl of snack mix, closed her eyes, leaned back and immediately went to sleep.

Ten minutes later, Mary Rose put a pillow behind her head and dozed off.

Marge finished her bowl of popcorn and lasted a full half hour before her eyes closed. A small stack of M&Ms was left in her bowl to eat later and enjoy just the chocolate taste.

Robbie took notes and munched popcorn and popped goldfish into her mouth until the caped toothy one had bitten the girl; then her pen dropped along with her eyelids.

Getting to Know You,
Getting to Know All About You

The next morning, Mary Rose made a run past the breakfast bar in the dining room, filling a plate with scones, muffins and donuts to take to Hadley's apartment for the second day of the Vampire Marathon. She got to the door the same time as Robbie who was carrying a bowl of fruit. Coming down the hall was Marge, with two big bottles of fruit juice. The red cane was draped over her arm.

"Hey Marge," Robbie grinned. "You're lucky. You don't have to use your cane much."

Marge grinned back. "Open the door, cookie. I'm ready for bites and blood." Robbie made a face at her.

But George Hamilton and *Love at First Bite* was going to have to wait. The girls were going to talk first.

It was as Hadley was pouring coffee – two separate pots, decaf for three, regular for one – that some of the hot liquid slopped over Mary Rose's cup. "I'm sorry," Hadley said. "What with all this damn macular degeneration I don't see well at all sometimes." And she grabbed a cloth and wiped up the coffee.

"She has to get shots in her eye and sometimes she faints," Mary Rose told Marge. "I don't blame her a bit. I'd faint, too."

Hadley and Marge both nodded.

Robbie looked at Marge. "You're probably the healthiest BOOB Girl, Marge." Marge did a quick look down at her breasts and Robbie smiled. "That stands for Burned Out Old Broads and you are one of us for sure with that cane. We're all thickened, seasoned women and we all have senior problems." She looked around at the others. "I have a tricky heart and have to go in and have it shocked into rhythm every now and then." She turned to Mary Rose.

"Breast cancer and arthritis," Mary Rose said, pointing to her missing breast. "And you know about all the time I spend in the bathroom!" She laughed. "Growing old sucks more than vampires."

"I've had uterine cancer," Hadley added. "As you get old you tend to fall apart, one part at a time. What doesn't hurt leaks. What doesn't leak creaks and what doesn't creak has probably been surgically removed." She sat down at the table with the other three and smiled at them. "We're like the old man who said, 'I may be old but I feel like a newborn baby; no hair, no teeth and I think I just wet my pants."

"Oh yeah," Marge nodded. "I have no gall bladder, no appendix, no tonsils and no sense. I have bad knees and no idea what's coming next." She paused for a second and they could tell she had just thought of something. A big smile crossed her face. "Speaking of ideas – Our local police unit brought a really old gentleman from the south in for questioning one time. I asked him if he had any ID and he said, ''bout what?'" And she laughed a good, rich laugh.

"You have met some interesting people," Robbie said.

"Real criminals," Mary Rose said.

Marge smiled again. "The most interesting was Weasel. They called him that because he could squirm into any place. He rescued me once.
"I had my left knee replaced and had to wear one of those super strong elastic braces over it. I called it TED - for Terrible Elastic Device. It was big. Covered this big old knee and went up above it and down below it. One morning I had showered and was in my bathrobe sitting on my bed.

I had just wrestled this elastic thing on and there was a terrible itch under it, right behind my knee. I couldn't scratch it through the elastic, so I reached in with my right hand.

"Now I'm sitting on the edge of the bed, so both knees are bent and as I tried to pull my right hand out of the elastic, my ring caught." She held up her hand with the enormous bright ring on it. "I tried everything. I couldn't get up. Put your right hand behind your left knee and try to stand up."

They did. They couldn't. They looked like four bent over turkeys bobbing up and down and laughing.

Marge went on. "Lucky for me, I could squirm around close enough to the dresser to reach my cell phone laying there. If I had called the station, my partner and half the detective squad would have come just to watch. I would have never lived it down. So I speed dialed Weasel. He's the best B&E man in Omaha and the little jerk had been my street informant for years."

Mary Rose spoke up. "B&E' that means Breaking and Entering." They all nodded.

"Weasel comes, gets through three locks on my door in about ten seconds, goes to my purse and takes out all my cash for payment, steps into the kitchen and pours himself a cup of coffee. Then he looks at me with my wet hair and in my bathrobe. He smiles, flips out his switchblade, cuts the TED off and leaves without saying a word, taking my favorite mug with him."

"Here's to the Weasel Man," Hadley said and raised her coffee mug. They lifted their cups and laughed again. "Laughing is good exercise,"

Mary Rose said with a big smile. "It's like jogging on the inside."

"Laughing isn't a *defensive* mechanism," Marge added seriously. "It's an *offensive* mechanism. When we can't laugh our soul shrivels up."

The fruit and muffins and juice were disappearing. They were laughing and patting each other now and then when something especially funny was said. Then Robbie got serious "What about your family, Marge? Are you widowed like us, divorced, have children? Fill us in, girl."

Marge leaned back in her chair and took a sip of coffee. She smiled a very tender smile that lit up her big face. "I'm law enforcement, I married law enforcement and I gave birth to law enforcement. One daughter is with the CIA in New York, another daughter is FBI at Quantico and a son is a detective in Chicago. My husband died years ago. He was a cop, too." She looked out Hadley's big window to the lawn below where borders of flowers were in full bloom.

"He died a long, hard death - cancer, heart disease, terrible lungs." She shook her head. "I came to truly understand the saying, 'It's sometimes more difficult to *see* suffering than *be* suffering.'" She sighed. "About four years ago I hooked up with a younger cop. He was sweet, but I'm not a very good Cougar. I never really knew what that meant, that word 'Cougar' for when an older woman goes after a younger man" She gave a little shrug. "Anyway, we broke up and he took my gerbil."

They looked at her.

"Your gerbil?" Robbie asked.

"Well, I thought I should give him something and Pumpkin was a very nice gerbil. She had a nice cage with exercise equipment and lots of toys. Her house was a little Cinderella castle."

"A cop with a gerbil and Cinderella castle," Robbie said. "You did right by him, Marge." Mary Rose did an eye roll.

Hadley reached over and for just a second touched Marge's hand. "As you well know, girlfriend, we never really get over death. We get through it. We move on. We keep on breathing in and out, but we never get over it. The sorrow becomes a part of us. It gets better. It gets different, but it never goes away."

There were tears in Marge's eyes "You know. I always said there were three categories of people in our lives: family, friends, and relatives. I'm not close to my kids. I have a sister I talk to once a year. But right now I feel like family." She looked embarrassed. The other three looked at each other and smiled. Eyes all around the table brimmed with tears.

"True BOOB wisdom," Mary Rose said. She stood up and motioned them all to stand, too. "Marge. You are an excellent friend and family and an outstanding BOOB girl. We need to teach you SHIT."

Marge's eyebrows flew up to her hairline, and she stood with the rest of them.

Robbie grinned. "It's an acronym." And she motioned for Mary Rose to go on.

Mary Rose, Hadley and Robbie stood very straight with good posture.

Mary Rose took a deep breath, "Shoulders back, Head high, Eyes (that's I) straight ahead, Tummy tucked in, SHIT. Whenever we see each other slouching or walking like old ladies, we just say SHIT and we straighten right up."

Marge laughed. "I thought it stood for Seasonal Hand Intensive Trauma," how your hands get cramps and sore from wrapping too many Christmas presents."

They talked on and on as good friends do. They told Marge about Maggie Patten, the original BOOB girl who named them the Burned Out Old Broads at Table 12, had taught them how to drive the Hummer and trailer, who had died on a cruise and how they had thrown her overboard for the burial at sea she wanted.

They told Marge about the other BOOB Girls; Calamity Doodles the little Ninja spy who had run off with BOOB Boy, Leonard, one of four Burned Out Old Bastards. The two of them ran away to re-join the circus just weeks after finding a hidden microchip in a gangster's mansion which Calamity later blew up.

They told Marge about robbing a grave, about Hadley's long-distance relationship with the handsome Indian sheriff, Wes Longbow. They even told her about Esmeralda St Benedict, the beautiful gypsy whose magic had let them dream wondrous dreams at Fort Robinson in out-state Nebraska.

Robbie cried when she told about leaving the Old Market after her husband died. Hadley went into the bathroom, brought out a box of tissues and plopped it down in the middle of the table.

Mary Rose grabbed one and told how her four daughters had moved her to Meadow Lakes without even asking her if she wanted to go. Then she laughed when she told them it was the best thing that ever happened to her and how she had made the four girls Christmas cards with Thank You letters in them. Marge Aaron was a very good listener. At last there was a pause, they looked at each other and smiled soft smiles. The morning had passed. Time had disappeared.

"Movie time!" Robbie said, and they headed toward the living room and a date with a vampire.

"You know what?" Marge said as they sat down. "Tomorrow for breakfast let's have a vampire drink: *Bloody Marys*."

Part Two

Boys will be Boys—Men Will Be Idiots

"And women will be crazy," Wiley Vondra thought.

Mary Rose McGill and Marge Aaron were having a Senior Texting Contest with their smart phones.

Mary Rose hit the tiny keys. "Get this one, Kiddo!" And she typed in BYOT.

Marge hesitated just a second. "Bring Your Own Teeth."

"And here's one YOU have to watch out for, McGill." DWI flew across cyberspace to Mary Rose's phone.

Mary Rose looked puzzled. "Something I have to watch out for." She thought for about five seconds. "Driving While Incontinent!"

"Here's one for Wiley," Mary Rose smiled and typed in "OMSG. Oh My, Sorry, Gas."

The Russians are Coming!
The Russians are Coming!

Wiley Vondra was still in a blue funk. He was sitting in the lobby of Meadow Lakes Retirement Community, which had neither meadow nor lakes, watching the fake fire in the tasteful, attractive fake fireplace. He was dressed in his usual jeans, boots, flannel shirt, brown leather vest and Stetson hat. In addition, he was wearing a whole bunch of miserable.

As he glanced out the window, a taxi pulled up. The driver and two young women in jeans and sweaters got out. The girls had pony tails and looked athletic and fit. The driver unloaded two big suitcases with attached wheels, the girls paid him and as he drove off they pulled the big suitcases up to the front door. Wiley stood, hurried to the door and held it open for them.

"Allo," the first girl said. "Ve haf come to vork." She looked around. "Eez these the Hilton in ze Old Market?"

Wiley smiled. "Nope. You got the wrong address. This is a retirement community. The

Hilton is several blocks east of here." He smiled and looked at them. "Where you from?"

"Russia," the second girl replied. "We come on study visa and will go to the University while we work." Her English was better. She appeared to be two or three years older than her companion. Wiley grinned. The girls' smiles lit up the whole room.

"Tell you what," Wiley said, pointing to the corridor just past the lobby. "You go down the hall there and the first door is the manager's office. Either John or Jane can probably take you on down to the Hilton. I'll watch your suitcases."

"Thank you. Theese is a nice place," the second girl said, looking around. "Maybe we will talk to him about working here instead of in dis hotel." And they stood their big suitcases up near the fireplace, smiled fetching smiles at Wiley and hurried down the hall toward John's office.

Wiley hadn't noticed two sets of eyes watching him until two older women were suddenly in his face.

"Who are those girls?" Adah Ashcroft said with a serious frown. She was a pretty woman who always dressed well. Today was no exception.

"They're from Russia and they meant to get out at the Hilton but they had the address screwed up."

Beulah Beckhaus was standing beside Adah. "Russian! They're Russians! There may be a **bomb** in those bags, Wiley Vondra. I'm calling the police." Beulah was short, stocky and dressed in early K-Mart.

Wiley had a surprised look. He grinned and shook his head. "For Pete's sake, Beulah, we haven't had the Cold War for years and why the hell would they want to bomb a bunch of stuffy old geezers?"

But Beulah was on a mission. She pulled out her cell phone and when Wiley turned to Adah he saw she had hers to her ear and was talking into it and gesturing back and forth and pointing to the big suitcases.

"Oh Crap!" Wiley muttered. Then he saw Zed Zonker hopping down the hall toward them,

cellphone to his ear, obviously talking to Adah.
They both shoved their phones into their
pockets at the same time.

Wiley didn't like Zed. He was an arrogant old
control fart, and Zed Zonker didn't like Wiley
Vondra either. He was jamming his big wooden
cane into the carpet and power-limping into the
lobby. He hurried up to Wiley and waved his
cane in Wiley's face.

"What are you up to, Vondra? Helping
terrorists now are you?" The cane was close
to Wiley's nose. He could feel the breeze from
it on his cheeks. Now Zonker was tapping
Wiley's chest with the stupid handle. Wiley
took a step backward.

"Christ, Zonker, they're just kids coming here
to go to school." Wiley reached out and grabbed
the cane.

That's when the bomb squad slammed through
the front door in full body armor.

A fire truck pulled up fast into the circle drive,
lights flashing, and stopped in front of the door.

A small crowd was gathering in the lobby. There was chatter and noise and shuffling around.

Adah and Beulah hurried over and started pointing out the suitcases to the bomb squad, the leader of which was beginning to smile. The two women were talking at the same time and bobbing up and down like lawn flamingos in a strong wind.

Two uniformed policemen came in the door just as the two Russian visitors came walking back into the lobby. John, the manager was close behind them. The lights from all the emergency vehicles were shooting color all around the walls.

"Is this where the party is?" John asked, looking around at the group who had gathered. Everyone quieted down.

After a short conversation with the head of the bomb squad, the girls opened their suitcases, smiled fetching smiles at the two youngest uniformed cops and laughed tinkly, attractive laughs.

The two policemen helped the girls close their suitcases, then they grabbed the big bags by the handles. The older officer turned to John. "We'll give the young ladies a ride to the Hilton."

There was total silence in the lobby.

The bomb squad left, unfastening their body armor as they went out the door.

The fire truck drove away.

Adah, Beulah and Zed disappeared along with the rest of the crowd.

John walked over and patted Wiley on the shoulder. "We haven't had this much excitement for a long time," he said, and he walked back to his office.

When Wiley turned around, Mary Rose McGill was standing behind him. "You want to go to my place and cuddle for a while?" She asked.

Wiley grinned. "You betcha! I haven't had this much fun in months." He took Mary Rose's hand and they started toward her apartment.

As they came to her door Wiley said, "Zed Zonker threatened me with his cane."

Mary Rose smiled. "I heard. And you got to have the police and a fire truck, too." She opened her door.

"Don't forget the bomb squad," Wiley said as he closed the door behind them.

Wiley Vondra didn't know it, but things were going to get a lot more exciting than Zed Zonker and his cane; more exciting than Russian girls and cuddling with his best lady. There was a new man coming onto the scene at Meadow Lakes. The original Fonz was about to change things.

Alphonso Greatwood

Alphonso Greatwood was big, black and boisterous. So was his electric scooter, designed for maximum mobility for the immobile.

The black scooter was a piece of art. For one thing, it had a red and orange roll bar over the top. Aluminum wings were attached to the front. Wild red and orange racing stripes – the same colors as on the roll bar – were painted on the wings.

A GPS was attached strategically to the front and a small pony saddle was mounted behind Alphonso's seat. "Bitch Seat" shouted from the little saddle in orange letters. In addition, he had whitewall tires and an unusually loud back-up signal that played the Nebraska Fight Song. When he went forward, which he liked to do at top speed, he pushed a button and played the theme from "Happy Days."

After all, he was the *original* Fonz.

It was a mean machine and that was its name. "The Mean Machine." From the day Alphonso Greatwood signed his contract to rent a one-bedroom apartment on the second floor of Meadow Lakes Retirement Community, he would become known as a holy terror and a traffic hazard.

Alphonso had been 25 years old when he signed with a new, first-year pro football team called the Kansas City Chiefs. He had a good career. No hall of fame bust, just consistency as an offensive lineman. As one of the greats had said, "My job is pluggin' holes." And Alphonso had plugged. He plugged until his knees were busted, his back cracked in two places and his helmet dented so many times it had knocked certain words right out of his head.

Even with a foggy brain and outlandish pain, he had been an MVP in more games than one, including a Pro Bowl. He was, in every way, a Most Valuable Player.

But losing words was what was most annoying. Hell, the knees and the injuries were just part of the game, but when he tried to think of a word, when his sentence was coming out just fine and then there was a sudden stop and the next word scurried away like a scared rabbit; that got to him.

Now all six feet six inches of him was stuck in a scooter and as sure as God laughs at old football players and racing stripes, Alphonso Greatwood was going to keep up his reputation and make sure he and the Mean Machine showed some personality.

It wasn't bad here at Meadow Lakes. In fact, it was downright pleasant. Alphonso realized that none of these nice retirement communities would admit it, but a big invisible banner hung over their front entrance.

Welcome! Now you're old.

No one saw the banner, but everybody knew it was there all right.

These communities were good places. Meadow Lakes had good food, the people were pleasant and while a few walkers and scooters were parked at one end of the dining room during meals, there weren't very many and a majority of those were temporary.

Some of the people here still went to work every single day and a good number did community volunteering. *Long shot from a nursing home*, Alphonso thought.

And the women! So many widows. Some were real lookers, too. When he'd played football there were women everywhere. Young. Busty. Narrow hips. Great legs. Groupies. And the players could have about any one of them they wanted.

Well, Alphonso had had his share and with a name like Greatwood he'd taken advantage of every rumor, every scandal and every joke about his having a Great Wood.

Unfortunately, that had changed. Now, as The Mean Machine zoomed down the hall toward the dining room, he wondered again why he had never married, never found the right girl, never even asked anybody. It was something he . . . searched for the word . . . *missed*. That was it. He *missed* never being married, never being anyone's most important person.

So it was with these rather sad thoughts that Alphonso Greatwood drove The Mean Machine into the dining room for his first breakfast at Meadow Lakes. He heard happy chatter, laughter and smelled eggs and bacon with just a tinge of the rich odor of ham thrown in. *Not bad,* he thought.

Across the room, Wiley Vondra looked up.
The men at his usual table were out for an
early morning golf game, so Wiley had brought
his plate to Table 12 and pulled up a chair by
Mary Rose. Now he was staring at the big man
driving his weird scooter around the tables,
looking for a vacant chair. Wiley's fork was
poised half way to his mouth.
"Sweet Jesus! Oh my god and holy moly," he
said out loud. "That is Alphonso Greatwood.
The Fonz, the Great Wood himself. Oh Sweet
Jesus, Sweet Jesus."

And Wily was on his feet, fork dropping to the
floor, hurrying as fast as he could toward the
big black man who had bumped his scooter
against an empty table and was stuck. Coming
full speed from the opposite direction was
champion power-limper Zed Zonker.

Wiley won. He made it to the big man's side a
full thirty seconds before Zonker and already
had him backed around the table and seated
before anyone reached them. Zonker took a
third chair and five other men hurried over and
surrounded the scooter and its occupant.

"Men!" Hadley said with an eye roll. "Who is that anyway?"

Mary Rose pulled out her smartphone. "Wiley said his name." She hit the little microphone that connected her to the internet and said, "Alphonso Greatwood." The phone chirped, then the screen was filled with sites on her search.

"Wow," Mary Rose said after tapping the first line. "He's NFL, Kansas City Chiefs. Most Valuable Player, Pro Bowl, all kinds of information." She read on in silence. "He's worth millions in bonuses. He's got his own website. He's famous."

They gave a quick glance at the man surrounded by other men. "Big guy," Marge said.

But while all the men were looking intently at Alphonso Greatwood, Alphonso Greatwood was looking across the dining room at Robinson Leary and he was looking intently, too.

Seduction by Ice Cream and Crabcakes

"The neat thing is," Marge Aaron was explaining, "is that I'm just a consultant. I'm retired and on a retainer. I'm just supposed to look around here, keep my eyes and ears open and see if anyone at Meadow Lakes could have murdered Perky Rasmussen."

They were just starting lunch and they were hungry after a good walk through the cemetery. They had left flowers from the Hy-Vee grocery at the graves of Mary Rose's and Robbie's husbands and in the mausoleum that sheltered the ashes of Hadley's man.

As was their custom, they put a single flower on Maggie Patten's husband's marker, not in honor of the husband, but in memory of their Maggie.

Marge went on, "I took the apartment here and after this case, I'm staying on. I love it here." She dropped her eyes to the table and picked up her coffee cup. "And I love you guys, too." She laughed. "I sound like a teenager with my VBFFs."

"Very Best Friends Forever," Mary Rose translated.

"I'll drink to that!" Robbie and Hadley said together. They began to dig into the asparagus casserole that had been served hot and steaming. Mary Rose sat facing the door.

"Here come Wiley and that Alphonso Great-whatever," she said, pointing toward the entrance to the dining room.

Wiley Vondra was walking alongside Alphonso's scooter and they were headed straight for Table 12. It was obvious they were on a mission.

"Ladies," Wiley said. He was grinning from ear to ear, which allowed a wave of relief to wash over Mary Rose. She'd been worried about his moods and what she considered a real depression.

"Meet Alphonso Greatwood, famous NFL player. Fonz, I want you to meet," and he began to point, "the lovely Hadley Joy Morris-Whitfield, the most powerful and personable Marge Aaron, the sweet Mary Rose McGill and," he paused, and grinned even wider. Bending at the waist, he actually picked up Robbie's hand and placed it in Alphonso's big paw, "Dr. Robinson Leary." Robbie and Alphonso were left awkwardly holding hands.

"Hi," Robbie said softly, pulling her hand away and smiling a friendly smile.

Alphonso wasted no time. "Dr. Leary," he said. He was hoping with all his might that his words wouldn't disappear. "I'm getting old and who knows how much time any of us have left." He took a deep breath and Hadley realized that everyone at the table was holding their breath as well. Then Alphonso blurted out his next sentence without breathing at all.

"Would you honor me by coming for ice cream at Ted and Wally's after lunch?"

He blew out his breath in a great sigh of relief that all the words had come out right or had even come out at all. Wiley grinned down at him like a proud teacher.

"Of course she will!" Mary Rose squealed.

"She'd love to." Hadley and Marge sat in silence, grinning at Robbie, their eyebrows raised. Robinson Leary finally, after at least thirty seconds, whispered a quiet, "Okay."

Hadley, Mary Rose and Marge watched through the dining room windows as Robbie walked beside Alphonso's scooter to his oversized, customized van. Robbie had on a light Creighton Bluejays jacket and Alphonso was wearing a Kansas City Chiefs sweater.

They reached the big van and Alphonso pulled out a remote control and clicked it. The back of the van swung open, a second click lowered a ramp and after saying something to Robbie that made her laugh, the girls watched him drive The Mean Machine up the ramp and disappear into the dark interior.

Robbie looked toward the faces in the window, shrugged, spread her arms in a "what am I to do?" gesture, waved and hurried around to the passenger door. The ramp rose into the van. The back door shut softly. The van moved down the driveway.

Omaha's Old Market was an attractive area near the Missouri river that drew tourists from throughout the world. The streets were brick; the sidewalks were shaded by both trees and wooden awnings that dripped beautiful, colorful petunias in the summer. Trendy boutiques and restaurants were in every long block along with an underground passageway that hosted even more good eateries and shops.

There were numerous art galleries and street musicians and at one corner horses munched oats while hitched to waiting carriages.

Ted and Wally's ice cream shop was in an old gas station on a corner. There were four hundred flavors that rotated each week. Robbie chose cookie dough ice cream in a small dish. Alphonso picked out a sugar cone with one dip of chocolate and a second dip of butter brickle.

They laughed when Alphonso told her about the different cities where the Chiefs had played. "If the end of the world comes," he'd said, "I… sure want to be in…..Louisiana." Robbie didn't seem to mind him losing words and hesitating to find them. As a result, he tended to lose fewer and hesitate less. He nodded. "I want to be in Louisiana when the world ends because everything happens twenty years later there."

She laughed. Alphonso thought both the ice cream and Robinson Leary were delicious.

Robbie pointed to the beautiful building next to the ice cream shop, the Mayfair, where she and her husband had lived in an apartment and where he had died. She told of loving the Old Market and missing the Farmer's Market on Saturdays and the beautiful Dickens in the Old Market at Christmastime when over a million lights decorated the downtown and characters from *A Christmas Carol* sang carols in shops and on the streets.

They strolled around the Eugene Leahy Mall, where water from the Missouri River was pumped into a canal that encouraged ducks and birds to feed. Robbie sat on an artsy chair shaped like a big hand and Alphonso found a pure white and perfect feather and presented it to her.

They had crabcakes at the Upstream Brewery which had, well over one hundred years ago, been the local firehouse. Built of solid brick and sturdy lumber, the huge doors were well preserved. From there horses had leapt into their harnesses and pulled the pump wagon through those doors and into the street, racing to any fire that occurred in the fledgling city. The streets were brick then, too.

It was time for dinner when Robinson Leary and Alphonso Greatwood got back to Meadow Lakes.

Both Wiley and Alphonso pulled up chairs at Table 12. Marge, who liked Alphonso's size and sense of humor laughed loudest when he told how, as a young man in Florida, he was tending bar when a friend came running in yelling, "Fonzie! Some S.O.B. just stole your pickup!"

"Did ya see who it was, Billy Joe?" he had asked.

"Nope," Billy Joe had said. "But I got the license plate."

The words came out just fine.

They all sat and talked for at least an hour after dinner, then they broke up to go to their own apartments.

Mary Rose looked at Robinson Leary and big Alphonso Greatwood and winked at Hadley and Marge. They both nodded and smiled. Marge gave a thumbs-up.

Robbie didn't wink or smile at anyone. She just went directly to her one-bedroom, walked straight to the bed, picked up the little brown and black bear sitting on her pillow and pressed one paw.

The voice of her dead husband came strong and sure through the gathering twilight, calling her his sweet chocolate, telling her how much he loved her. The other paw held a tiny recorder with her mother's voice.

She began to cry before she could press the other paw and she wondered how a woman old enough to collect social security checks could still miss her mother.

The BOOB Girls are the Good Girls

Robbie and Alphonso spent a lot of time together, and while Wiley seemed to be pouting about his new best friend running out on him, Alphonso was all bouncy, teen-age happiness. He gave residents rides in the Bitch Seat on his scooter. He took a van load of new friends to the museums and to the famous Omaha zoo. One weekend he took Robbie on what he hoped was a romantic trip to Kansas City to see the Chiefs play.

It had been a fun but confusing trip for Robinson Leary. They were guests in a huge skybox with food and drink and fame. People came by to shake hands with the great Fonz. The ESPN announcers recognized him and asked him into the press box to comment on the game.

Before they left, after the game was over, players came to greet him. Robbie's neck was sore the next day from looking up into the faces of so many tall, big men. "Most of the time, I could have talked into their chests," she told Alphonso as they drove home.

Robinson Leary wasn't sure she liked football. She was glad to get back to Meadow Lakes.

"He owns his own fame and is proud of it," she told the girls as they walked down the hall to the Meadow Lakes Bistro.

The Bistro was a small, cozy room with a glass wall and door opening into the dining room. It held a coffee machine, a popcorn machine, a soft-serve ice cream machine and two ice cream tables. It was cheery and pleasant and as they approached Mary Rose said, "It's good to claim and own your talents and your personality."

Hadley agreed. "I own my own dignity," she said.

Robbie joined in. "I own my own intelligence."

"I own my own innocence," Mary Rose added.

They looked at Marge who was quiet for just a minute, then she grinned.

"I own my own gun," she said.

They laughed and Hadley gave Marge a quick hug while they walked into the Bistro. Hadley headed for the soft serve ice cream machine and before she could pull the handle to create an ice cream cone she heard Marge say, "Shit!"

They straightened their shoulders, held their heads high, eyes straight ahead and tucked in their tummies. All three of them realized at that same time that Marge wasn't reminding them of their posture. Standing at a distance outside the Bistro were the two detectives, What and McGill.

Baggage Claim
or Never Trust A Suitcase

What had on his Columbo coat and McGill's hair was looking more and more like a dead bird in full molt. They walked into the Bistro before the girls had time to sit down.

What didn't even acknowledge them before he started to speak. He was obviously excited.

"Three years ago yesterday, Maggie Patton washed ashore at Geezer Point, just outside Mutant, Washington."

He smiled a wicked smile. "If you are going to dispose of a body, you don't tie it to suitcases in the middle of a storm at sea. Suitcases catch the currents and the next thing you know, bingo! Some kid is making sand castles and the Avon lady shows up.

"Only it wasn't a kid. It was group of those End-of-the-World folks waiting for Jesus. Well, Jesus didn't show but Maggie Patten did. They worshiped her for two weeks in a Winnebago trailer in Mutant while May 13th came and went. No end of the world except for Maggie

Patten." He had said it all in one breath and now he sucked in new air like a vacuum cleaner.

He looked like Garfield the Cat after a big meal of fat canaries. "So there she was. How did she manage the belt around the suitcases by herself? She didn't, did she? No. No Siree."

They all stared at him. It was a horrible storm and Hadley, Robbie and Mary Rose all had vivid memories of wrestling Maggie's body over the railing of the ship, watching it balance on the rail on the deck below, then finally roll into the roiling, wind-driven ocean below.

"It's been a long week and McGill's eye is tired, but it sees all and so do I. You thought you'd get away with it didn't you?"

"And so . .????" said Hadley remembering similar confusing moments with tax accountants.

Detective McGill took a step forward and eyed them with his one eye. "So...." He said. "We think there may be a connection between Maggie Patten and Percolator Rasmussen."

"You've got to be kidding," Robbie said. She noticed that Marge had moved closer and was holding her cane in one hand.

Detective McGill spoke, slowly. "Maggie Patten washed up on Geezer Island on May 13th. Percolator Rasmussen was murdered on May 13th and on top of that, the world didn't end on May 13th. There's a connection. And somehow it's connected to you old women who are really nothing but Burned Out Old Broads."

Mary Rose jumped to her feet, moved face-to-face with the other McGill and frowned a huge frown. "This is an APE! An Anxiety Producing Experience. And listen to this, Buster."

Hadley leaned toward Robbie and Marge, "Did she just call him, 'Buster'?" They nodded. A sweet, half-smile was creeping its way onto Marge's face.

Mary Rose went on. "Shorty . . . you need a break. And don't ever call us 'old women' again! You bet we're old, but we're beautiful. Just look at us with your good eye.

"Our faces are sculpted by sorrow and tears and laughter. Our hair is blown thin by the winds of experience and we have so much wisdom and knowledge in our heads that we don't have room for it there. It's trickled down through the rest of our bodies and that's why we've gotten thicker. NOT FAT. *Thicker.* And another thing….."

When Mary Rose McGill got on a roll, she really got on a roll. She took a deep breath and looked at her friends. "You're right. We're old. Our *children* have AARP cards for Heaven's sake! Just remember, we don't like being old so it doesn't take much to tick us off!"

She moved to a chair and sat down, visibly out of breath. Then she noticed everyone else was on their feet. She immediately got up and stood with the other girls who were all grinning.

Everyone was quiet. Then Hadley leaned up to Robbie's ear and whispered, "Our Maggie rose from the sea like Venus."

"Mary Rose was actually poetic," Robbie whispered back. They continued to grin.

Marge had heard them. "Venus de Avon Lady, Worshipped in a Winnebago. What a way to go...and to come back, for that matter."

What and McGill looked downright disgusted. They sniffed, gave the girls a dirty look and turned together toward the door leading to the lobby and on to the parking lot.

Suddenly Marge held her red cane straight up in front of her. She pressed one of the big jewels and a cloud of pink gas shot out of the cane, flew through the room and exploded on What's butt.

A horrible smell of rotten eggs filled the entire room. Mary Rose coughed. Hadley waved her hand in front of her face and Robbie covered her mouth and nose. Marge smiled and gently put the red cane back on her arm.

"What," McGill whispered loud enough for them to hear. "You should never expel gas in public."

"I didn't you idiot, it was you!"

"Nonsense. I have no gas. I am gas free."

"You are a monstrous gas bag!"

And they scurried out the front door. The girls could see them still arguing as they walked to their unmarked police car.

They all turned toward Marge and her red cane.

"Like I said," she smiled. "I own my own gun."

Rose Gardens and Super Bowl Rings

Marge Aaron sat straight as a rod at Table 12, her arms crossed, her eyes glaring at the person seated across from her.

She was, to say the least, as intimidating as a rhinoceros. That glare had made wife beaters wither. That glare was what every mother wanted because, as Marge would tell us, it reduced her children, who were CIA, FBI and Chicago PD, to sniffling seven-year olds. And now that glare was focused on Dr. Robinson Leary.

"OK, girlfriend," Marge said. "We know something is going on. You come out here in the morning and you've been crying. We walk the cemetery and you're quiet until you come to your man's grave then we're drowned in a waterworks. You look as hang-tail as Wiley Vondra on a bad day." She paused for effect. "Talk!"

Robbie sighed and looked at her three friends. "I'm a bad person," she said softly.

They leaned forward to hear better.

"Alphonso wants to get married. He says he loves me and he's never been in love before." She smiled a sad little smile. "Actually, what he said was, 'I've never loved a bean before,' but I knew what he meant."

Mary Rose broke in. "Are you in love with him, Robbie?"

The Fonz and Robbie had been together every day since they'd been introduced, and every night Robinson Leary had cried herself to sleep.

"I love him," Robbie said, her head hanging. "But I'm not *in love* with him.

"But that's not the problem. If I marry Alphonso I'll have no financial worries ever again." She smiled a weak little smile and gave Hadley a friendly slap on the arm. "I could buy you out, rich girl."

They were quiet for a minute and Robbie pointed to the far end of the dining room where a television crew was shining bright lights on Alphonso Greatwood and a local television sports caster. "He's famous," Robbie pointed out. "He has a great sense of humor, he's kind, he's generous, he's so vulnerable with all his trouble with words….."

"There's a 'but' coming, isn't there?" Hadley said.

Robbie nodded. "BUT –" . A tear rolled slowly down her cheek. She nodded. "But," and she took a deep breath and said very fast, "he's in a scooter and I don't want to have to take care of another incapacitated man." She blew her breath out. "There! I've said it. I feel guilty about it. I'm a bad person."

"Like hell you are," Mary Rose piped up, louder than she intended.

All three women's eyebrows shot up. Mary Rose McGill never swore, but Mary Rose McGill was getting braver and braver.

"You have a right to your own life, Robinson Leary. You weren't put here to be a slave. Your great grandmother was a slave and I bet she didn't like it. If you married Alphonso pretty soon you'd be getting all kinds of things for him from the refrigerator, you'd be driving the van, you'd be helping him dress." She paused and leaned toward Robbie. "By the way, is he well-endowed?"

Hadley's eyes got as big as saucers. "Mary Rose McGill!" she said.

Mary Rose looked right back at her. "Well, I wondered," she said.

Robbie smiled, "I think so, Mary Rose, but we haven't gotten to the naked stage and at my age, I don't plan to do so in the near future."

Marge Aaron did an eye roll. "You can't give yourself away, Robbie. You've been there, done that, paid your dues and you don't have to do it again.

"There's no reason you can't keep things just the way they are and if something develops and you fall madly in love, there you are. And if you don't, there you are. You're the one in charge of your own relationships, just like Alphonso is in charge of his." She shugged. "If they meet, fine. If they don't, that's fine, too."

"Well," Robbie sighed and looked at her friends. "In my faith I've always believed the

Holy Spirit lives in the air and when you get things out in the open healing takes place. I feel a little better now. I'm going to tell Alphonso we need to slow it down and that I'm not willing to get married. We can be close friends and love each other without being married. Then he can own the relationship he wants. If it's too different than mine, adios Alphonso."

As she finished speaking, the television lights at the end of the dining room went off and Alphonso and the Mean Machine headed toward Table 12.

The dining room was empty now except for the five of them. As he got closer, Robbie got up and walked toward the big black man and his Mean Machine.

He stopped. She pointed to the big doors leading to the gardens outside. Alphonso grinned and patted his Bitch Seat. Robbie gingerly climbed on and wrapped her arms around his huge chest. She laid her head gently on his equally huge back and they headed toward the dining room exit and the blooming gardens on the outside.

Dr. Robinson Leary didn't look back.

Men!

Now Wiley Vondra and Alphonso Greatwood were *both* depressed. They moped together. They pouted together.

Wiley walked alongside the Mean Machine as Alphonso drove around the Meadow Lakes property. Wiley gestured wildly and Alphonso did the same with one hand. They were obviously plotting something, but neither one would come within shouting distance of Table 12.

And when Mary Rose knocked on Wiley's door after dinner one night he – not very politely – told her to go away. He was busy. It was a better silent treatment than most women were capable of giving.

Then it all came together.

Hadley Joy Morris Whitfield literally ran, as fast as she could manage, into her apartment where she would have total privacy and made a frantic phone call to Wes Longbow, the retired sheriff.

"Wes!" she almost yelled into the phone when

he answered. "You have to come right away. Wiley's in trouble. He's in jail."

Wes' voice sounded annoyed. "I can't come right now, Hadley. I'm in the middle of a big consultation involving three counties. There's no way I can get away. Just tell me what happened and I can maybe talk to Wiley or at least make some phone calls for you."

Hadley took a deep breath. "He and Alphonso tried to rob the La Viva Crypt, that bar a couple of blocks away, the one that's owned by that creepy funeral director."

"I know the place." Wes said. "Modesty Liam is the bartender, hostess, manager and long-term girlfriend of the funeral director, Morgan Graves. She has a Great Dane named Digger." Wes laughed a sharp laugh. "Her name may be Modesty but everybody calls her Moezy Liam so it sounds like Mausoleum." Hadley could tell Wes was thinking. "They have great drinks there."

Wes seemed to be lost in remembering the bar and not the least bit worried about Wiley Vondra.

"They have the usual Bloody Mary, of course, but they have Embalmer's Fluid which is Scotch on the Rocks and they have the Undertaker, that's the house Margarita – they have little bones in the drinks instead of umbrellas, and their beer – God, is it good – they call it The Walking Dead. And you know what we should do next time I'm there, Hadley? We should all go down and have Slabs and Bones, that's their burger and fries."

Hadley squeaked. "Wes Longbow! Listen to me! Wiley Vondra is in jail and so is Alphonso! And how do you know all about La Viva Crypt anyway?"

"What do you think Wiley and I do when I'm there and you BOOB Girls go off on your own? We go to the Crypt and have a drink. But you say Wiley tried to rob the place?" Now she could hear the surprise in Wes' voice.

"Yes. He and Alphonso. They went in. Alphonso had a gun and a bag to put the money in." Then and there she felt her face start to turn red.

"Wes, I don't talk like this. I don't use this kind of language and I don't approve of it, but – I'm quoting now – Alphonso gets his words mixed up sometimes and," she took another breath, drawing it in through her clenched front teeth.

"He looked at this Moezy woman and said, 'OK mother-sticker, this is a fuck-up.'"

She hung her head. "I'm sorry Wes, but that's what he said." Hadley plopped down on her bed, holding her phone tight against her cheek.

"Then, instead of handing the bartender the bag to put the money in, Alphonso handed her the gun. Wiley asked if they could please have the gun back and this, Moezy, you called her, said, 'No way, Jose,' and she fired a shot through the ceiling, breaking a vase in the apartment above the bar and scaring a cat so badly it still hasn't come out from under the bed. And the poor dog, you called him Digger, ran into the back room and pooped all over the place."

She knew Wes was covering his phone and laughing. She could hear him.

"It's not funny!" she said.

"Actually, Hadley, it is. But who's this Alphonso character."

"He's an old football player who's been hit in the helmet way too many times. Alphonso Greatwood."

There was a moment of total silence, then Wes' voice broke through. "Alphonso Greatwood! The Fonz! The Great Wood himself? Man, Hadley, he's Pro Bowl MVP. He's got a super bowl ring.

Alphonso Greatwood! Don't worry, honey, I'm on the next plane. I'll see you in a few hours." And he hung up.

Hadley looked at her phone, shook her head and put the receiver in its cradle. She rolled her eyes.

"Men!" she said out loud.

Part Three

Gary's Song: To the tune of I Enjoy Being A Girl

I am a scary Vampire
With my teeth sharpened every day
If you don't want me to bite you
You'd better run fast away.

I am a frightful Vampire
With a white face and lips blood red
I would just love to nip you
And make you so very un-dead.

I am a fashionable Vampire
With a coffin tre' stylish and more
I sleep well every day there
Martha Stewart did all the decor

I'm Gary. I'm scary.
I'm scary. I'm Gary.
I'm Gary, the Vampire Man.

A Guy has to do what A Guy has to do

Modesty (Moezy) Liam may have had tattoos
over more than half her body (one was of seven
coffins the colors of the rainbow stacked on top
of one another).

She may put a little too much blue eye shadow
on the corpses she dressed and made up at
Billow DeGround Mortuary, Crematory and
Monument Sales, but her hair styles were
known all over Omaha as the best for the dead.

Most important of all; she liked Wiley Vondra
and Alphonso Greatwood. She liked Wes
Longbow, too, but thought of him as one very
old cowboy.

When questioned about the caper pulled by
Wiley Vondra and Alphonso Greatwood,
she told police it was all a prank and that
Alphonso's gun had gone off accidentally when
he was handing it to her.

That was a small white lie but it kept Moezy
out of the slammer. The young couple in the
apartment, who were pushing bowls of food
and water under their bed for their cat, were

pressing charges. Wiley and Alphonso were doomed to a sleepover in the Douglas County jail.

Marge Aaron made a few phone calls and introduced herself as a retired homicide consultant, but the young policeman who took two of her calls didn't believe her and when she called the chief himself she got an answering machine.

Mary Rose McGill and the other girls thought the boys deserved the sleepover behind bars and refused to post bail. What was even worse, Wes Longbow couldn't catch a plane until early the next morning.

Alphonso had to sit on a too-small cot that pinched his butt when he sat on it and tortured his back when he tried to lay down.

He and Wiley had a cell of their own since Alphonso was handicapped, but they took his scooter away and not one of the guards or other prisoners was old enough to remember him. It was humiliating.

Wiley was so upset he couldn't sleep so he kept Alphonso awake all night.

The first thing Sheriff Wes Longbow did when he got to town was to take a cab to Meadow Lakes and hug Hadley. She tended to be more forgiving than Mary Rose McGill who put her sweet Catholic girl hands on her hips and said, "They deserve what they get!"

Robbie tended to shrug, look at Mary Rose and do eye rolls. Marge Aaron was introduced and Wes invited her to come with him to visit the apartment dwellers with the broken vase and scared cat. Professional courtesy.

The young couple in the apartment above La Viva Crypt were named Luci and Ricky. They obviously were not happy about bullets flying through their floor, but as soon as Marge sat down, the cat came bolting out from under the bed and jumped on her lap.

Luci squealed, grabbed her kitty and said everything was all right now. The cat, which was one of the ugliest Marge or Wes had ever seen, growled at its mistress, struggled out of her arms and jumped on Marge again.

As so often happens, Marge hated cats. She considered it a noble sacrifice for Alphonso and Wiley that she stroked the dumb feline, said stupid things like, "Nice kitty, kitty," and even asked what the cat's name was.

"Mandu," Luci beamed. "As in Katmandu, the city in Nepal." Luci giggled a high-pitched giggle. "Get it? Cat Mandu."

Mandu was looking at Marge with big, mean kitty eyes. He definitely planned on staying on her lap. It wasn't until he started to pee right there on her legs that Marge jumped up and pushed Mandu off onto the floor.

"Oh, I'm so sorry!" Luci squeaked. She had an irritating little girl voice and Wes Longbow was having fantasies of going downstairs to the bar, ordering a strong Bloody Mary and shooting his own pistol through the ceiling.

Instead he stood and said, "It appears everything is all right here. It was an accident, after all and Mr. Greatwood will be happy to not only pay for a new vase and the repairs to your floor, but he is also prepared to provide a year's supply of premium cat food for sweet Mandu here"

Now it was Marge Aaron's turn to do an eye roll.

Luci and Ricky and Mandu agreed not to press charges.

Wes and Marge visited the jail and brought Alphonso and Wiley back to Meadow Lakes with them.

Both of the hardened criminls met all the womanly demands of men who have done something stupid.

They were contrite.

They apologized.

They were humble and ashamed.

They were the envy of every man at Meadow Lakes Retirement Community.

Wes Longbow finished his consultation through Skype, emails and telephone calls and was staying for a week with Hadley.

Wiley had become so important in his circle of men friends that his depression lifted and he was heavy-duty into paying attention to Mary Rose McGill.

Robbie felt sorry for Alphonso and took him to Ted and Wally's for ice cream and spent an entire afternoon at the zoo with him.

Marge Aaron did some serious detective work because Percolator Rasmussen's murder was still an open case. It was while she was once again walking around the neighborhood for any kind of insight or clue that she found something very strange and interesting.

The Mean Girls

Each of the girls got a phone call from Marge telling them to meet her outside the front door of Meadow Lakes.

The big doors opened onto a long circular drive that led to the sidewalk. Without saying a word, Marge motioned for them to follow her.

She began to walk to the sidewalk. When she reached it, she turned left then began to cut through the woods that bordered the retirement community.

"Where are we going?" Hadley asked.

Marge shook her head and put her finger to her lips. They began walking slowly through the thick trees, careful not to trip over roots or branches. The woods were shaded. The trees dripped darkness, even in the midst of a sunny day and dry leaves crunched under their feet.

Robbie looked around her. They were walking single file now because the trees were so thick and close together. "The woods are lovely, dark and deep, but I have promises to keep and miles to go before I sleep," she said softly.

Hadley, walking in front of Robbie, turned and smiled. "Robert Frost. **Stopping by the Woods on a Snowy Evening**. One of my favorites."

"I trust we're not going miles before we sleep," Robbie whispered back.

In just a few minutes they came to a tumble-down little house. It looked as if it had wanted a paint job for years.

The lawn was weed-filled and an old porch that had once wrapped around the little house was half gone, some of its little pillars hanging loose, dirt-covered and looking miserable.

The windows were encrusted with years of dirt and several shingles had blown off the roof and were lying in random spots throughout the yard.

Marge made her way to the front steps. The girls looked at them and shook their heads, then Marge took the first step.

As soon as her weight was on the boards of the step it caved in beneath her. "Yikes!" she said, pulling her foot out. Something live scurried away and hid in the dirt under the porch.

Marge tested the second step, found it secure and hopped awkwardly up. She made the porch with one more step and the other three followed – carefully. The old wood creaked under their weight.

Marge looked around at them and knocked on the door.

Nothing.

She knocked again, louder.

Still nothing.

Then a sound came from inside.

"Shhhhhhhh. Click, Creak. Shhhhhhhhh. Click. Creak."

Marge put her ear to the door. Robbie leaned in. "What do you hear?" she whispered.

"I hear Shhhhhhhh. Click. Creak." Marge whispered back.

They all moved to the door and put their ears against it. Suddenly the door flew open and all four girls stumbled inside.

Standing there was the oldest woman any of them had ever seen. She was in a walker. She turned her back to them and began to scurry like a little animal across the floor. The rubber tips on the walker gave out a shhhhhhhh sound as she moved it forward. The woman's legs gave a click sound. Her ugly, skinny ankles provided the creak.

The crowded little living room looked as if it had been decorated by a demented social worker.

There was a huge television that looked like it came from Tiger Tom's Sports Bar.

An oversized couch sat in front of the TV. A recliner sat on each side of the couch.

Magazines were in piles on the floor, most of them grocery store tabloids. On one table next to the television were two piles of DVDs.

Robbie moved closer, bent down and read the titles. "*Buffy the Vampire Slayer*, all eight seasons," Robbie said.

Marge looked up. "Buffy only had seven seasons."

Robbie reached down and held up a DVD. It was in a pure black cover with "Buffy: Season Eight" written in white along the spine.

There were stacks of horror films. Robbie looked further. "I love their Stephen King collection," she said. "He's stacked next to **Murder She Wrote.** They have the entire series. Wow." A tiny spike of envy tore through the heart of Robinson Leary.

A full two minutes passed before the little woman returned. Following her were three other extremely old ladies, all dressed in white model coat house dresses and white orthopedic shoes. Their white hair was messed and one had her hair in spikes all over her head. It was obvious she had a glass eye.

"We should introduce her to detective McGill of the one good eye," Hadley Whispered to Robbie.

Only one of the women wore any makeup and that was just a slash of bright orange libstick smudged across her lips. "I think they stopped making that shade in 1950," Robbie whispered back.

"Ladies!" Marge said, pulling out her badge. Her red cane had not left her arm and now she held it tight against her side while showing them her credentials.

The lady of the orange lipstick peered and squinted then nodded. She looked straight at Marge. "'Bout time," she growled. The old ladies were standing close together, side by side.

Mary Rose moved close to Hadley. "Are we looking into some kind of mirror of the future? They could be us twenty years from now."

"Make that twenty-five," Hadley said. "We don't look that bad."

The four women looked at them, then Orange Lipstick spoke. "We are The Mean Girls." She began to point her friends out, one by one. "I'm Mable. This is Myrtle, that's Mildred and here's Fred."

"Mabel, Myrtle, Mildred and Fred?" Robbie asked.

"Milifred," Mabel replied. "She doesn't like that name." Robbie nodded and Milifred cackled like a chicken. Myrtle's glass eye stared at Marge while her good eye squinted at Mary Rose.

"We're investigating the murder of one Percolator Rasmussen," Marge said. Before she could say anymore, Myrtle began to jump up and down.

"We did it! We did it!" She spun around in a circle and ended with a neat little curtsy.

Hadley watched the glass eye in case it popped out.

"And exactly how did you do it?" Marge asked.

Robbie noticed for the first time that even though the couch and chairs were leather, there were crocheted doilies on the back and arms of each. It reminded her of her grandmother's house years ago except Grandma was a neat freak and these ladies had never had an affair with Mr. Clean.

"Percolator Rasmussen. I bashed him in the head with this!" Mabel said, walking to a non-working fireplace and picking up the small shovel used to gather ashes.

"I cut his throat with a butcher knife from the kitchen," Fred said. She started toward the hallway but Marge's voice stopped her.

"No need to show me, Fred. I believe you." Fred stopped in her tracks, turned and came back to the other Mean Girls.

"I strangled him with our handy-dandy-over-the-bathtub clothesline," Mildred chimed in.

"Myrtle?" Marge asked. "What did you contribute?"

"I did the old knife-in-the-back trick," Myrtle said. "Then we put him in an old coat that belonged to Mildred's dearly departed husband. He was involved with some unsavory characters in Chicago and his suit coat ended up with a most unfortunate and unattractive bullet hole. More unfortunately, he was in it at the time." Mildred, the dearly-departed's widow, gave a high-pitched giggle and plopped down in one of the recliners. No one else sat.

"Then you dragged him over to Meadow Lakes and deposited him in the dining room?" Marge asked. They all nodded.

"We are The Mean Girls," Mildred said. "We are the Spawn of Satan."

"We are children of the Dark One," Myrtle added.

"Daughters of the Cloven Hoofed Lord," Mabel nodded.

"Seed of the Devil himself," Fred finished

Hadley and Robbie looked at each other. "Same father, different mothers," they said together.

"You can't arrest us!" Fred continued. "Perky was evil. He was a vampire and a pervert." She took a deep breath. "We were sitting on our porch steps one time and he exposed himself to us."

The BOOB Girls looked at them.

"He walked up in front of us wearing this old raincoat," she went on. For some reason, Marge Aaron thought of detective What and his raincoat, but she immediately cancelled any thoughts that might have followed.

"He came right up and opened up his coat and showed us his privates," Myrtle said.

Tiny Mildred wore the weirdest expression Mary Rose had ever seen.

"It was terrible, "Mildred said. "I had a stroke. Myrtle had a stroke. Mable had a stroke." Then she cackled. "Fred couldn't reach that far." They all said it together like it was a rehearsed joke. Hadley couldn't help smiling; she heard Robbie chuckle and Mary Rose gasped. The Mean Girls cackled away.

"Why would he expose himself," Marge asked, still the detective.

"To distract us!" Myrtle yelled. "He was a vampire and he would have bitten us and sucked our blood, little of it as it is. We can't spare any. We're old. We have weak blood. We're all anemic."

While Myrtle was talking, Mildred slipped over behind the television. When she came out she was holding a rifle and it looked to be in perfect working order, obviously the cleanest item in the room. She cackled and the other three joined in again.

"Haul ass!" Marge shouted pointing to the door.

They hauled ass.

As they hurried down the steps, Hadley caught her foot and fell flat. Robbie stumbled and fell on top of her. The four Mean Girls were following them out the door. Mary Rose pulled Robbie then Hadley up from the ground. They turned to see Marge press a jewel on her red cane. The air filled with a thick fog that surrounded the Mean Girls.

"I can't see!" Mildred shouted

"I'm blind!" Myrtle yelled.

"We're defeated!" Mable roared and she threw the walker at them. It sailed through the fog and bounced off Mary Rose's shoulder with a clatter and a thud.

"What is this?" Mary Rose yelled, holding her shoulder and looking at the red cane. "Deadly weapons of the elderly?"

"We're outta here!" Marge hollered and she grabbed both Robbie and Hadley by the arms and started running into the woods. Mary Rose passed her in a flash and reached the trees first.

"Ow! Ow! Owie!" Hadley said when they were safe inside the darkness of the woods. "I skinned my knee when I fell." Her slacks were torn and her knee was, indeed, bloody.

"I'll put some iodine on it when we get back and it will hurt worse," Marge said, grabbing Hadley and pulling her along.

"Ow! " Hadley said again.

They hurried to Meadow Lakes and upstairs to Hadley's apartment as fast as they could go. Hadley sat on her couch and Marge got iodine and band aids from the bathroom. Robbie knelt and blew on Hadley's knee while Marge cleaned it, put on the iodine and band aids then sat down with a monstrous sigh in one of Hadley's chairs. They were all still puffing a little.

"They killed Perky!" Mary Rose said.

Marge shook her head. "No. They couldn't drag his body over here and all those things weren't what killed him. I got a leak from the medical examiner's office and if the leak is true, it's an even weirder case."

Mary Rose pointed to Marge's red cane.

"Marge. It's time you told us about this cane."

They all looked at it.

The sun, pouring through Hadley's window made the jewels sparkle and dance. Marge opened her mouth, but before a word could come out, Wes Longbow and Wiley Vondra sauntered in the door. "Door was open," Wes said. "Where have you girls been? We want to go down to La Viva Crypt for slabs and bones,"

He saw Hadley's torn slacks and bandaged knee. "Honey, you're hurt." He sat beside her and put his arm around her.

"Owie," Hadley said. She gave him a pitiful look. "Owie, owie, owie." Robbie, Mary Rose and Marge shook their heads and rolled their eyes.

Welcome to Billow DeGround Funeral Home, Crematory and Monument Sales

Marge had left right after breakfast to meet with her liaison downtown. Wes had wiped his mouth with his napkin and followed Alphonso and Wiley out the door. They were headed to Lincoln, Nebraska, the home of the University of Nebraska because Alphonso could get them all box seats just to watch the Cornhusker football team practice with a tour of the weight room thrown in.

"What do you want to do?" Hadley asked Robbie and Mary Rose, but before they could answer, John the manager walked up to Table 12.

"I need help, girls," he said. "Jane is with the grandchildren. Today I have an all-day seminar, Stephanie is swamped and Ruth is out getting supplies." He sat down. "The medical examiner is ready to release Perky's body and since he has no family I'm afraid it falls to us to make burial arrangements."

They stared at him. Mary Rose's mouth hung open for a second, then snapped closed. Hadley stared and Robbie frowned.

"There's that funeral home just a few blocks from here, Bill Billow and Dusty DeGround built the ugly monstrosity about four generations ago according to some of the old gentlemen here. Would you go down this morning, pick out a casket for Perky and we'll pay for his burial."

They stared at him some more. No one said anything.

John stood, smiled, patted Robbie's shoulder and said, "I knew I could count on you. I'll never forget how you got him to drop his pants and drawers and hop around and then convinced him you could tell his age by looking at his junk."

He smiled and shook his head. "And you'd just been to his birthday party a day or so earlier."

He patted Robbie again and walked away.

"He's blackmailing us." Hadley said.
Robbie nodded.

"Yep," Mary Rose said. "I always felt a little guilty about doing that to Perky. Let's go visit the freaking funeral home."

Billow DeGround Mortuary, Crematory and Monument Sales was exactly six blocks from Meadow Lakes.

The girls walked. It was a cloudy morning, with greyness hanging all over the sky. "Good day to go to a funeral home," Robbie commented. Hadley and Mary Rose were quiet.

The big, ugly Victorian-style mansion that housed the old funeral home was, appropriately enough, next to a sign that said, "Dead End. No Turn Around."

Where years ago stately funeral homes had lined Omaha's Farnam Street and occupied blocks that became known as Funeral Home Row, Billow DeGround sat alone and lonely. They stood on the sidewalk and looked at the creepy old hose.

"All we need is a bat flying out of that big tower on top," Mary Rose said, looking up.

"Let's all sing The Adams family Theme when we go in," Robbie remarked

Hadley just looked at the big house and shook her head. "Crap," was all she said.

They moved up the sidewalk, ignored the handicap ramp and took the steps to the huge front porch. They stood in front of the huge wooden double doors and rang the bell.

"Doesn't work," Hadley said after she had tried it twice.

"Three time's the charm," Mary Rose said, reaching over and pressing the doorbell.

Nothing.

Robbie shrugged and opened the door. Just as the door creaked opened, a huge black grandfather clock standing in the foyer began to strike ten. They jumped. Then they laughed.

"Beautiful clock," Hadley said. "Ironwood I believe. Rare." She looked at her friends. "Expensive."

There was no one around; no receptionist's desk, no greeters, no funeral director.

A large portrait hung next to the clock. It was of a serious man with a shock of grey hair. Beneath was a plaque that read, "Morgan Graves: Proprietor."

Mary Rose turned around. "Mr. Graves!" she yelled at the top of her voice. Robbie and Hadley both jumped a little. "Mr. Graves!" Mary Rose yelled again.

Nothing. They were greeted by a haunting silence.

She turned and shrugged. "Well," Hadley said, "Let's go looking."

"Why does that sound ominous?" Robbie asked.

"He probably has an office down the hall," Mary Rose suggested.

The only thing down the hall was a door marked, *Caskets*.

"That's what we're here to pick out," Hadley said. And she opened the door. It creaked.

"Is this a Nancy Drew Moment?" Robbie asked.

"If it is," Mary Rose replied, "We need at least one exclamation point!"

An overhead light came on automatically and they heard the scurrying of tiny feet. "Mouse or rat," Hadley said.

"As long as it doesn't bite," Robbie said.

"Yish," came from Mary Rose.

The entire room was lined with caskets of all kinds. There were cheap cloth-covered ones, stylish metal ones and glorious wood ones.

Hadley looked around. "Did you know that in New England they have Casket Barns where funeral homes keep the caskets in actual barns apart from the funeral home itself?"

"Really?" Mary Rose said.

"More information than you needed, but I spent some time in Maine one year. Learned stuff." Hadley went on.

"Stephen King lives in Maine," Robbie informed them.

"Hadley looked at them. "Shit!" she said, and they straightened their shoulders, held their heads high, put their eyes straight ahead and tucked in their tummies. "We were slouching," she explained.

"I suppose we need to get the cheapest one," Mary Rose said, moving toward a cloth covered casket. "Perky won't care. He's dead." She pointed to a cloth-covered casket near her. "The lids are all raised with prices taped inside."

Robbie looked around. "Which one would you two pick for yourselves?"

Hadley and Mary Rose looked around.

Mary Rose walked toward a lovely pink metal casket. "This one is for me for sure. But dress me in red so I'll stand out." She gave a nervous little giggle.

Robbie walked over to a light oak casket. "I like this one. And you can dress me in a black pantsuit with a brown turtleneck the same shade as this box. I want to be coordinated."

They all laughed and things were less tense.

"You can put a glass of good pinot noir in my hands," Robbie added.

Hadley moved to a mahogany casket partially hidden in a little alcove against the far wall. "Look at this one! I bet it's the most expensive one here. This has my name all over it."

She stood next to it and rubbed the shiny wood on the top. "All the others are open with their lids raised. I wonder why this one is closed."

The other two girls moved in beside her.

Robbie bent down and looked, then felt all around the lid. "I don't think it's locked."

She moved to directly in front of the casket, put both hands under the edge of the lid and tried to raise it. "Yuk. I'm a wimp and a weakling."

Hadley and Mary Rose came alongside her and put their hands under the edge as well. "Okay girls. On three," Robbie said. "One…..two….. THREE!" and they all lifted with all their muscles.

The lid flew open.

Lying inside, looking up at them and scowling was a slightly pudgy young man in black jeans and a plain black t-shirt.

They jumped back so fast that Robbie lost her balance and crashed into the closest casket. Hadley grabbed Mary Rose and stepped back, her mouth open, eyes wide.

"Jesus, Mary and Joseph!" Mary Rose said. And she made the sign of the cross.....twice.

Gary the Vampire

The man sat up, turned, looked at them and literally sprang out of the casket.

"You can't even get a good day's sleep around here anymore." He looked at them, hovered together holding on to each other. A sly smile came across his pox-marked face. "Well, well. The BOOB Girls from Table 12. How cheery."

Hadley straightened up. "How do you know who we are and what are you doing in my casket?"

"It's not *your* casket. It's mine. Take a look. It's personalized and has Martha Stewart pillows."

In spite of the scare and surprise, they moved closer and looked into the mahogany box.

Sure enough, there was a photo of a family from the 1940's pinned to one side, a picture of Dracula taken from a movie magazine and fresh flowers lying near the little embroidered pillow. There was a decorative throw folded neatly at the foot and a lovely walnut box about eighteen inches long lying along one side. It looked downright homey. They began to relax a little.

Robbie was first to speak. "Very nice," she said. "Are you Mr. Graves catching a quick morning nap?"

The man laughed. He was barefoot and just a little taller than Robbie and Mary Rose; not quite as tall as Hadley. His black hair was combed straight back, greased down and he was unusually pale. *Not a lot of time spent outdoors*, Hadley thought.

"I'm not Morgan Graves. I'm Gary. Gary the Vampire." And he slammed the casket closed and jumped, in one smooth move, on top of it, sitting facing the girls.

"There are no such things as vampires," Robbie said. "I've researched them."

"You researched movie vampires," Gary said. "I know. I hang out around Meadow Lakes a lot.

You four have more fun than anyone else there. I follow you around sometimes." He smiled a rather pleasant smile. "Only in the evenings, though. I can't imagine how much you do in the daytime."

"So you're a vampire," Robbie said, moving closer to him. "Let's see your fangs, then." Gary was definitely more interesting than frightening.

He hung his head for just a second, then looked at Robbie with sad eyes. "That's my problem." He hesitated then looked at each of them, "I have dentures."

Hadley couldn't help it. She laughed out loud. "A vampire with dentures?"

Gary gave her a dirty look and nodded. "Bad teeth before I was bitten and changed."

Just a note of defensiveness crept into his voice. "But I'm trendy now. Janet Evanovich had a toothless vampire in one of her books. He had to gum people to death."

"He was a demented old man who only *thought* he was a vampire," Robbie said. "And you must be a demented young man who thinks he's a vampire."

"Oh, I don't just think it. I am one."

Robbie shook her head. "No self-respecting vampire is named Gary."

"What! You did all the research and you think we're all Slavic with names like the great one, Dracula. Or Lestat? Holy Garlic!

"Didn't you read the **Twilight** Series. They have Edward and one of those cute cozy mystery writers has a vampire named Bill.

"You think Edward and Bill are OK and not Gary? And how about Johnny Depp! He's Barnabas Collins in **Dark Shadows**! What kind of vampire name is 'Barnabas?'" His face was getting paler instead of redder as Hadley would have expected.

The vampire named Gary was on a roll. Since he'd spied on the BOOB Girls for years, he felt he knew them and it was high time he unloaded his woes on somebody.

He jumped down from on top of his casket, zoomed over to a screen that stood against one corner of the room, reached behind it and zoomed back carrying four chairs.

"Have a seat. I'm sorry I can't offer you anything to drink, but we don't allow refreshments in the casket room. Good fabric here, you know."

They sat. Robbie thought if this was a movie she'd cast the other Gary, Gary Sinise in Gary's role instead of the young man sitting beside her.

She liked Gary Sinise and she wasn't sure about this Gary guy. Her mind wandered off a little and she thought how she could write a vampire TV series called *The Young and the Lifeless.*

"I was bitten and changed in the 1940's," Gary began. "Gary was a very popular name then. They all three leaned toward him and squinted. He definitely wasn't around seventy years old. He was really demented.

"I had a wonderful girlfriend named Hedy. She was little. Cute as a bug. She was bitten and changed at the same time."

Here he paused and looked at the floor. "You'll understand this because you're women. She was bitten just before her period and she was bloated. Now she has to go through eternity bloated. She's pissed." He kept his head down.

Mary Rose held up her hand. "I relate."

Gary looked up. "So she hasn't spoken to me for sixty years. I don't even see her anymore."

"That's sad," Hadley said. "We're sorry, Gary." Strangely, she was starting to believe him.

"I resent the vampire who changed us," Gary said. "It was Dr. San Guinary from **Creature Feature** and he could have waited. Just because he was a big TV star he thought he could do anything."

"I remember him," Hadley said with a note of excitement. "He was terrific, but he was more of a zombie creature than a vampire. My granddaughter showed me a really neat current website about him."

"The zombie thing with the white coat - that was really his vampire clothes. He was fashionable and very well dressed. He became famous after he changed us so he wasn't such a hot shot at the time." Gary slapped his leg in frustration.

"OK, vampire with a common name, helps me with my research. You live here, in the funeral home?" Robbie was finding this fascinating.

Gary nodded. "It's a perfect place for a toothless vampire. What do they do in funeral homes? They embalm bodies. How do they get embalming fluid into the body? They drain out all the blood. I can feast here all I want. Graves does a pretty fair business."

Mary Rose crinkled her nose and said, "Yuk."

"No yuking." Gary said back to her. "It's good most of the time. Sometimes we get somebody who's had to take a lot of meds and I get a real druggie high. Sometimes Graves gets a drunk who's been run over and there's an alcohol fix for me. One time he got a rich old dude who had a heart attack after drinking a good brand of Scotch. That was awesome."

They were looking at him with their mouths open.

"Will you burn if you go out into the sun?"
Mary Rose asked. Her voice was as innocent as
a child and it was obvious she was enthralled.
Hadley was interested, too.

"No. That's a myth," Gary shook his head.

"Stephanie Meyer in **Twilight** got it right.
We kind of sparkle. And now of course
America overdoses on sunscreen. But we're so
noticeable we can't go out much." He looked
thoughtful. "Since you're not leaving, I'll tell
you what I do in the daylight." He looked
directly at them, one at a time. "I'm a Vampire
Slayer."

He paused for effect and waited. It hadn't quite
had the stunned reaction he had hoped for.

"How can a vampire be a vampire slayer?"
Robbie asked.

"There are evil vampires," Gary said. "They
suck people dry and you'll never suspect them.
I know who they are though. Evil smells
different."

"How do you slay them?" Hadley asked.

"Usual way," he smiled and pointed to Robbie for the answer.

"Stake in the heart?" Robbie guessed.

"Bingo." Gary nodded. "Stake in the old ticker. Works every time."

"Let me get this right," Robbie said leaning forward in her chair. "Morgan Graves lets you live and you eat, or drink as the case may be, here and sleep in the casket?"

"You got it. Morgan is old and sometimes he knows I'm here and sometimes he doesn't. He hasn't quite figured it out yet.

"Sometimes he thinks I'm his night watchman.

That's cool. He's also almost totally deaf." Gary tipped his chair back and put his hands in his jeans pockets. He grinned. "Now Moezy, his young assistant and main squeeze, she knows about me. She's a sweetie. Works at the bar Morgan owns on the side."

"La Viva Crypt," the girls all said together.

Gary kept on grinning and nodding.

"Graves is so unaware and so deaf. One time I came home early in the morning, sparkling and everything. He was mowing his lawn wearing his suit.

"I went up to him and yelled, 'It looks really nice, Mr. Graves.' He didn't miss a beat of the old rotary mower. He just nodded and said, 'Yes, well, she was sick a long time you know.'

He thought I was talking about a body he'd just rolled out for viewing." He gave a short and rather pleasant laugh. Then he turned serious.

"I have really enjoyed having you here. You can't imagine how lonely it gets."

"The only people I know are the four witches who live at the end of the woods and those ladies are craaazzzzy!"

"The Mean Girls?" Mary Rose asked.

"You got it," Gary said. "I think every day that if I could just get a regular job, one without a lot of stress where I could be around a lot of people, I could be happy for the rest of the century. But I have no contacts, no network. I'm not even on Facebook."

"Gary, are you about to cry, Sweetie?" Hadley's voice was full of empathy. Gary sat up straighter in his chair and smiled a sad smile. "Would if I could. Vampires don't have tears."

"There are no such things as vampires," Robbie insisted, but not as strongly as she had at first.

"That proves I could handle a job and be around people," Gary said. "Nobody believes in me so nobody would notice me. I'm like that cellophane man in the song from Chicago."

"I love Chicago," Mary Rose blurted out. "I liked the movie better than the play."

"Me too," Gary said. "But now I have to bite you and change you. I should kill you, but I like you and Graves has trouble handling more than two bodies at a time."

"You can't bite and change us," Robbie said, getting a little testy. "What are you going to do, gnaw us?"

They all three looked at Gary and realized he was serious. His face was set and when they thought about it, he was probably right. They could be a real threat to him, undead or not. At the same time, Robbie and Mary Rose made a dash for the door. Gary was there ahead of them, his back to the door his hand behind him turning the lock.

Hadley stayed where she was and slipped her hand deep into her pocket. She felt for her cell phone, pushed the button on top to open it, pressed what she hoped was the little phone symbol, then pressed what she hoped even more was Wes Longbow's speed dial number. She could hear the faint ringing and held her breath. Was it true that vampires had super hearing?

One ring. Two. Three. Four.

Come on Longbow! Answer the damn phone!

"Hello, there," Wes' voice came loudly and happily from her pocket. His phone was telling him it was Hadley on the other end.

Gary spun around. "What was that?"

Hadley kept her hand on the phone and took a step forward, "I said HELLO! I mean HEL-LO. What do you mean you have to kill us or change us? Nobody knows we're here at Billow DeGround Funeral Home, in the Casket Room, being held hostage. What do you think's going to happen, Gary Man, that someone is going to come bursting through that door at the end of the hall and rescue us? Well, that would be nice if someone would, but do you know anybody who would come fight for us?"

She could tell Wes had pushed the end call button. She just hoped he got everything she said.

"If you just let us go, we won't tell anyone you're here," Mary Rose said in her most innocent voice. Then she thought for a second. "But we still have to pick out a cheap casket for Perky unless you want to do that after we're out of here. Think on it, Gary. Just relax and let us go."

Gary shook his head and moved away from the door, down near Hadley and his casket. "Nope. Won't do it. Wouldn't be prudent. A guy's gotta do what a guy's gotta do." Gary sighed. He reached into his pocket and pulled out a little instrument. He held it up for them to see.

"That's a lobster fork, for Pete's sake," Hadley said, moving over beside him. "You're going to stick us with a lobster fork?"

"I only have to get a little blood and you'll change into a vampire. If I drink a lot, you die, and I really don't want you to die. I've never killed anyone or anything except evil vampires, and they're not human anyway. You can even pick where you want to be stuck, a pick stick sort of thing."

Mary Rose walked over near him. "Gary, you don't have to do this. We won't tell anyone and we'll come visit you. We could get you a dog or a cat, something to love you."

Robbie moved next to Hadley. "Would you be interested in writing a TV series with me? I was thinking of making it about vampires. We could call it, **The Young and the Lifeless.**" Gary looked at her. "That's from a website talking about Johnny Depp and Tim Burton and **Dark Shadows.** You can't just go around stealing other people's titles even if it's said as a joke.

Damn! Robbie thought.

Hadley moved back to her chair and motioned for them all to sit down. "Before you fork us, Gary, I'm interested. What kind of job would you like if you could have one?"

He spun the little lobster fork in his hand and looked as if he were lost in a memory. "I grew up in Boothbay Harbor, Maine."

The sad smile was back. "You say it Boothbay Hah-bah when you're a Main. When I was in high school I washed dishes in one of the café's on the wharf. I loved it. Simple job. Simple, honest people. Hard work……" he went on.

Hadley guessed about four minutes had passed. She hoped Robbie had some more questions. But it was Mary Rose who bought them time.

She started to cry. "I wish you were my son. I have these four daughters who don't care enough about me to even send me a lobster or a lobster fork, let alone stick me with one……"

Gary was listening and nodding, leaning forward toward a weeping Mary Rose McGill, looking kindly at her while she traced an imaginary rosary with her hand. Hadley breathed a short sigh of relief. Once Mary Rose got started, there was hope.

Red Canes and Mean Machines

Just as Mary Rose was drying her tears on Gary's handkerchief the cavalry arrived, and it wasn't what Hadley had imagined.

She had hoped Wes Longbow would rush through the door, gun drawn and lead them all to safety. Instead, the door crashed to the floor and in flew Alphonso Greatwood on his Mean Machine. Seated on the bitch seat, her legs straight out to the sides, was a very angry Marge Aaron. Hadley noticed the tires on the scooter were nearly flat from their combined weight.

Marge held her cane in front of her, pressed a jewel and an electric charge from a taser shot into Gary's body.

"Ow! That stings." Gary didn't go down.

Wes Longbow, who actually did have his gun drawn, was stepping over the fallen door and rushing to Hadley's side. Wiley Vondra literally jumped over the door on the floor to get to Mary Rose. Robbie just got out of the way. Marge was on a rampage.

"Take that, you little squirt!" And she hit another jewel that turned the cane into a gun.

A bullet went through Gary's arm but no blood spurted out of the wound.

"Will you quit that!" he yelled at Marge.

"Not on your life – or lack of one," Marge yelled back and she pushed another jewel and small pellets shot out around Gary's feet, making him lose his balance and do a macabre kind of dance.

Marge grabbed the end of the cane and pulled out a long, thin yellow rope.

"Wonder Woman on steroids," Robbie said, leaning as close to Hadley as she could.

"The Golden Lariat," Hadley said back. It was obvious Marge intended to tie Gary up. Gary, in the meantime was turning around, facing his casket.

Marge hit another jewel and knives sprang out all over the cane. She awkwardly climbed off the scooter, nearly fell, then turned toward the vampire.

Gary saw the knives. "Oh, for Dracula's sake!"
He said.

His voice sounded annoyed and disgusted.
He gave them all a mean look, scowled and
growled at Marge, then in one quick movement,
zoomed into his casket and closed the lid. They
could hear the click of locks being engaged
from the inside.

It was completely quiet. Dust motes lingered in
the air.

Robbie moved to Alphonso, put her arm
around his big shoulders and kissed his cheek.

"Thanks for crashing the party," she said.

Wes still had his arm around Hadley's shoulder
and his gun at his side as they moved toward
Gary's casket.

Mary Rose was holding tight to Wiley's hand
and Marge and Robbie were side by side.

They encircled the casket. Marge held her cane
ready to fire whatever she planned to fire from
it.

Wes had his revolver ready. He reached out with his other hand and tried to lift the lid.

Marge added a hand and soon all of them were pulling and panting, but the lid wouldn't budge. It was locked tight from the inside, all right. "I suggest we get out of here," Wes said. "The authorities can handle this." And he started toward the door, followed by everyone except Hadley. She was still standing beside the big mahogany casket.

"We can't just leave him here. He's scared and angry and.....and demented"

"Hadley, it's not for us to do. We need to get the police. Come on, we're all going. Let's go to the Crypt or Happy Hollow and have a nice glass of wine."

"Or a Walking Dead beer," Wiley added.

Hadley Joy Morris Whitfield crossed her arms and glared at the two men. "*Fine*! You go ahead."

Wes looked at Wiley then at Alphonso who had Robbie settled neatly in on his bitch seat. "Fine is the most frightening four-letter word a woman can say." He took a step back toward her and said, "What do you want to do, Hadley?"

She didn't answer. Instead, she turned to the casket, put a hand on it, tilted her head near the lid and said, "Garrrr-eeeee:"

No answer.

"Garrr-eeee."

Still no answer.

"Garr-eeee," she said a third time.

"What-eeee?" finally came from inside the casket.

"What if I could get you a dish washing job? Would you come out, be good and not stick anyone with your lobster fork?"

There was a long silence, then they heard locks being released.

Happy at Happy Hollow

It was the next evening. The day had been overcast and gentle sprinkles came and went throughout the afternoon. Because of the cloud cover they were able to go, with an excited Gary the Vampire, to Hadley's country club in west Omaha.

Dinner had consisted of the weekly pasta bar, a favorite of Hadley's ever since her husband had joined Happy Hollow Country Club and golfed there every week.

The wine selection was exquisite and the conversation had been laugh-filled. Gary, of course, had not eaten. He was not even at the table with Marge, Wiley, Mary Rose, Wes, Robbie, Alphonso and Hadley. He was in the office of Ryan, the banquet manager who, without knowing it, was having an actual Interview with the Vampire. Ann Rice, eat your heart out.

Wes was pouring the wine when Kelly, the clubhouse manager came up to the table.

Jim, the general manager had stopped by to say hello and had commented on Hadley bringing in yet another good employee for the club.

Dorothy, the longest-term employee had come and sat with them and made sure there was a plate of cookies on the table for dessert.

"We just hired the young man you brought in, "Kelly told Hadley. "He seems nice. He's awfully pale though, I hope he isn't sick."

Hadley shook her head. "Not so you'd notice."

"He's got a great sense of humor," Kelly went on. "He joked about being a vampire and said a club this big must have a lot of bloodsuckers, too. He seems to love washing dishes and having a night job. What's really helpful is how he's so fluent in Spanish." Hadley looked at Robbie, who looked at Mary Rose, who looked back at Hadley.

"Well, if he doesn't work out, dear," Hadley said, taking ahold of Kelly's hand. "Just drive a stake in his heart and call it a day."

The Medical Examiner

Marge Aaron came hurrying toward Table 12. Breakfast was over. The dining room was emptying out and earlier, Robbie, Hadley and Mary Rose had all tried calling Marge. She had not answered her phone for anyone. She sat down with a plop and a sigh, standing her red cane gently against the table.

"It's some kind of cane," Robbie said, looking at the jewels twinkling in the sun that was beaming through the big windows of the Meadow Lakes dining room. "Who made it?" Marge laughed. "If I told you that, I'd have to shoot you." She caught her breath and leaned toward them. "The medical examiner is coming by. She accepted an invitation for coffee and I knew she'd like you girls. She's quite a BOOB Girl herself." Marge leaned back in her chair.

"She knows what killed Perky."

They were all quiet.

"We never did see Morgan Graves to make burial arrangements," Hadley said.

"Not to worry," Marge said. "The examiner's office will take care of it. He had no family, so there's not much to do."

A car door slammed. A large, black SUV pulled up near the front door. A good-sized, attractive woman in a Nebraska Cornhuskers jacket, red turtleneck and black shoes and slacks got out.

She had light brown hair with just a touch of grey at the temples and her walk was straight and determined. She was obviously a woman of confidence and ability and she was coming through the door and looking at Table 12.

Marge stood up. The other three followed suit.

Marge gave the newcomer a warm hug, then introduced her. "Nancy Southern, these are the BOOB Girls I was telling you about; Hadley, Robbie and Mary Rose."

Mary Rose spoke up. "Nancy Southern? Do you have a sister named Clarabelle who owns a nudist RV park on Nebraska Highway 2?"

Nancy Southern put her head back and laughed a rich, melodious laugh. "She's my sister, all right, and we even look a little bit alike. Same father, different mothers."

Nancy Southern was likeable. She pulled up a chair and joined them. Ruth, the activities director came in the dining room, grabbed the pot of decaf, came to their table with a smile and an additional cup for Nancy and refilled their coffee, leaving the pot on the table.

Marge patted Nancy's arm. "Nancy is one of the best ME's in the country. She makes Kay Scarpetta look like a wuss and a wimp."

"Scarpetta has too much angst," Nancy said with a wink.

"She makes Bones on TV look like a teenager."

"Bones on TV IS a teenager," Nancy smiled.

"And as for Megan on *Body of Proof,*..." Marge just pointed to Nancy Southern this time.

Nancy took a sip of her coffee and leaned toward them. "Megan is too beautiful. That's the trouble with TV medical examiners as well as TV female detectives. Look at their hair for Christ's sake! They all have hair that takes two hours a day just to groom it. They have perfect make-up and they wear pointed-toe high heels. They're obviously actresses playing serious roles." She pulled a strand of her hair straight out.

"Look at this. It's short. Minimum maintenance. I work a good twelve to fourteen hours most days. I'm in a super cooled room that smells of disinfectant. I'm on my feet all the time. If I wore high heels I'd be walking on stumps because my feet would fall off. And those women are all pencil thin. That's because they spend so much time with their hair and clothes and make-up and shopping for shoes they don't have time to eat." She leaned back and laughed again.

"We like you!" Robbie said.

Marge smiled. "And you still have some hours to put in today, girlfriend, so thank you for taking your break with us and for coming by.

Here's the big question: How did Percolator Rasmussen die and who killed him?"

Marge took a breath and another drink of coffee. Ruth came by again with a tray of cinnamon rolls and left them on the table, checked the coffee pot and went for a refill.

"The back of his head was smashed in. Probably by a shovel or a baseball bat." The girls looked at each other. They were all thinking of the little shovel at The Mean Girls' house.

"His throat was cut, more than likely with the same knife that was stuck in his back." More thoughts of Mabel, Myrtle, Mildred and Fred.

"There was a bullet hole in his coat, but he hadn't been shot." The husband in Chicago who met some unsavory characters.

"And the nylon cord around his neck was from one of those little clotheslines you put over your bathtub." That pretty much sealed it. The Mean Girls.

"But none of those things killed him."

"Say what?" Robbie said.

"Like I said. None of them. What killed him was….and this is where we get a drum roll if we have a drum….what killed him was a stake in the heart."

There was a united gasp from three of the four BOOB Girls at Table 12. Marge didn't know about Gary's claim to being a Vampire Slayer. Shades of Buffy herself.

Mary Rose touched Nancy's wrist. "What about his feet? What and McGill said his toenails had been trimmed and someone had rubbed oil on his feet." The others had forgotten all about the foot fetish of the two detectives.

Nancy shook her head. "Apparently he took tremendously good care of his feet. He obviously went barefoot a lot. Of all the things about Mr. Rasmussen, I have to say his feet were definitely number one. We should all take better care of our feet, actually." She nodded, smiled and sipped her coffee.

Nancy Southern, Douglas County Medical Examiner, looked at her watch. "As to who did it? We don't know. There was no blood in his body. He'd been drained someplace other than here, killed someplace other than here and dragged from someplace other than here."

She looked at them and smiled again.

"I'm tempted to joke about it and say it's the most complete case of suicide I've ever seen, but that's a joke and I don't joke about suicide. It's a tragedy and I pray for the families who experience it. At least we don't stigmatize it anymore and bury the victims at crossroads or outside of cemeteries. We've learned too much about mental illness to blame the victim."

Nancy Southern got up. Looking at her the girls had good memories of stopping at her sister's clothing-optional RV resort on their way to Ft. Robinson a year ago. Bare Essentials RV Resort had welcomed them, housecoats and all, to a truly wonderful breakfast with good people.

"Do you ever get to Bare Essentials to visit your sister?" Mary Rose asked.

"I do indeed," Nancy smiled. "One thing about being clothing optional, you don't have to pack a heck of a lot. I have a college-age daughter,

Mary, and she loves it there." She shook hands with all of them, gave Marge one more hug and walked proudly out the door.

"I really do like her," Mary Rose said. They all nodded. None of them mentioned Gary and his claims to killing evil vampires.

Epilogue

And so our story ends, as all stories must. Troubles have come and gone. Worries have worn themselves out, as worries do. There has been adventure and newness to life, even to those sheltered away in retirement communities. Friendship has endured and grown, expanded and encompassed.

Since he had packed light, Wes Longbow went to Parsow's Fine Clothing in Regency Fashion Court and bought a suit.

He took Hadley to V Mertz, her favorite Old Market restaurant located in the beautiful passageway between two sets of buildings. She wore a new pink suit with low, silver heels and matching purse. She sat facing the passageway and watched all night for the Old Market vampires Gary had told them about. She didn't see any.

Mary Rose and Wiley got back to serious cuddling and Wiley's depression lifted after the adventure at Morgan Grave's funeral home. He came to realize how precious life had become as he had grown older and also how precious Mary Rose McGill was to him.

Robbie and Alphonso spent good time together. He drove her to Louisville, Nebraska, because she wanted a new purse from Coop de Ville, one of the most delightful shops in the whole state. He bought her the purse and a beautiful necklace and earrings, which she thought was much too expensive to accept, but she did so anyway because it made him feel good.

Early one morning the girls put on good walking shoes and traipsed through the woods to the little house where they had found The Mean Girls.

They took travel mugs of coffee with them, sat on a rock on a little hill behind the house and watched. They didn't see anyone and there were no sounds or activity coming from the cottage. It appeared to be empty.

The walker Mabel had thrown at them still lay in the yard, lonely and waiting for rust. After Mary Rose had dashed into the bushes to pee, they got up, stretched and made their way home.

Gary loved his job at Happy Hollow and the people there loved him. Once on his night off he and other kitchen workers went to Benson, one of the little villages that make up the greater Omaha area, and paraded in a Zombie Walk.

But after work and play, Gary went back to Billow DeGround and his mahogany casket. He lay down on his side, reached over and picked up the beautiful wooden box the girls had noticed when they looked into the burial box. He smiled, opened it and took out a beautiful, long stake. It was pencil thin, its polished wood shone in the little nightlight he had fastened to the lid of his coffin. He looked at the dark stain that covered the sharpened tip and thought how it gave it such a lovely contrast.

There it was. Just a hard-working little stake. As for Marge Aaron; she did not disappear into a dreamy fog as did Esmeralda St Benedict the gypsy.

She did not join the circus like Calamity Doodles had done, and she did not end up with a burial at sea along with Maggie Patten. No, Marge Aaron was here to stay.

While Robbie and Alphonso were at a movie, and Wes and Hadley were dining in style at V Mertz, and Mary Rose and Wiley were in the laundry room playing poker while Wiley washed his clothes, Marge Aaron sat at Table 12 in an empty dining room, polishing her red cane.

In front of her on the table was a letter from the good and strange Detective What.

Dear Marge,

Thanks for the retirement watch with bloody severed hands for the hour and minutes. Wow, where did you find that? What a gift and reminder! Speaking of reminding, tell the crew at the station that the jar of loose change in my desk drawer is 35 years of what fell out of pockets at crime scenes. Tell them to use it for the Christmas party.

McGill and I are in Florida still trying to get that last case out of our minds. It keeps coming at us. It haunts us. Would you believe that down here in Florida someone is trying to sell "Vampire" brand sun screen? "Night in a Bottle." That is its slogan. Then last night McGill and I had dinner with a

woman who is advocating for "Transfusionists". .
.cross species children of Vamps and humans. She
had the senior class picture of one that looked
like a one fang Zombie with a chain saw look
in his eye. We gave her $50.00 for a "Go Suck"
prosthesis fang. Sports model I guess.

Anyway, I will keep you posted on our efforts to
open our salon. "What and McGill" just sounds
better than "McGill and What." Makes me feel like
a curiosity.

Must go. Thanks again for the watch. Clever how
they got it to only tick and not have a tock. Sounds
like a time bomb on my wrist.

Yours in crime for the big bucks,

What

Marge cleaned the many jewels on the cane
until they sparkled.

She checked the batteries on the Taser and on
the pellet gun and made sure the pistol in the
cane was cleaned and loaded.

She sharpened the knives and rewound the lariat.

Marge Aaron smiled to herself.

She hummed a chorus or two of *I Enjoy Being A Girl.*

And as she polished and caressed her nice little weapon, she thought what a great title it would make for the next book:

The Red Cane

**A glass of bubbly champagne,
a big bowl of BOOB Girl popcorn
and more to:**

*Dr. James Campbell, known to those who love him as *Slick Sheetz*, is one of the loves of my life. Jim created and wrote in the great detectives, What and McGill. Jim is also the author of several good books, the latest of which is *The Holiness of Water*. Visit his neat new website: www.wonderuntobeauty.com

* Meg Noyes, the classy lady whose name graces one of the librarians.

*Ada Miller whose brother gave us the true account that became *The Russians are coming! The Russians are coming!*

* Colleen Kelly, my high school classmate who had adventures with knees and TED.

*Dr. Susan Adams whose knee is a classic.

*Pour a Walking Dead drink to Debi Oliver who created everything we know about La Viva Crypt and its menu. These menu items may be found at Debi's house.

*Nina Picolo gets the best casket in the room for revealing how Gary the Vampire was changed and for bringing Doctor San Guinary, a favorite Omaha character back to life, creepy as it may be.

* A creepy good wish from Mildred, Myrtle, Mabel and Fred to Cindi Peery, who is anything but mean but who wanted mean girls in the book.

* Beautiful Kelly Smith, who is the gem of Happy Hollow Country Club and Ryan, the dining room manager who hired Gary the Vampire deserve a huge plate of the club's delicious cookies.

*My favorite reader, daughter Jenny Ritter who would add a dog to every book if she could and would do it right.

*A high class new purse display rack to Dr. Liz Cochran of Coop de Ville in Louisville, which really is one of the best gift shops in Nebraska with some of the best snacks anywhere.

*To my daughter, Janet Sieff, heartfelt thanks for all the good suggestions and the covers in the series, but especially this one.

*Paris Sieff, who took the terrific photo on the back and whom I'm lucky enough to claim as a beloved granddaughter.

*A gold feather carved into a pen gets lovingly presented to Marc Roberts, Ben Schroeder, Louise Vance and my husband Marv for finding my many typos and inconsistencies. We left some typos for your amusement and to let you have a feeling of superiority.

* A free weekend at Bare Essentials Clothing Optional RV Resort to my friend Nancy Sothan, who turned out to be a really good medical examiner.

*Love and hugs to all of you who allowed me to annoy your group and give my BOOB Girl speech.

*I googed and googled, but could not find where the great statement, "May you laugh so hard tears run down your leg," came from. But I thank you whoever you are, and I wish that to all of you reading this.

* The handsome old dude who is my personal Wes Longbow, Dr. Marvin Johnson deserves a

big hug and wet kiss for all the driving, taking credit cards, being the only man in the group and especially for loving me all these years. He continues to hope the series will get picked up by a big publisher so he can be a genuine gigolo.

* Pour a glass of champaigne for the great Phyllis Diller, who kindly endorsed the series and who is Queen of the Burned Out Old Broads.

*And a special thanks to all of you who shared ideas, love and laughter. I know I have forgotten some of you in this thank you, but I will never forget you in my heart.

About the Author

Joy Johnson is over 75 now. With her late husband, Dr. Marvin Johnson, she founded Centering Corporation, North America's oldest and largest bereavement resource center, and Ted E. Bear Hollow, Omaha area's center for grieving children. Joy has written or edited over 100 books on grief, many for children. After she retired in 2009, she began writing **The BOOB Girls**: The Burned Out Old Broads at Table 12, a comedy-mystery series for senior women.

Joy has three children and six grandchildren. She lives in Omaha, Nebraska, with her husband, Ted Brown and a tabby cat named Margaret Thatcher. Like her characters, she is a funny, active beautiful BOOB Girl.

If you enjoy this book, you'll love and laugh with:

The Boob Girls:
The Burned Out Broads at Table 12

The Boob Girls II:
Lies, Spies and Cinnamon Roles

The Boob Girls III:
Sandhills and Shadows

The Boob Girls IV:
Murder at Meadow Lakes

The Boob Girls V:
The Secret of the Red Cane

The Boob Girls VI:
From the Eye of the Moose

The Boob Girls VII:
Ten Little Puritans

The Boob Girls VIII:
Learning to Love Willie

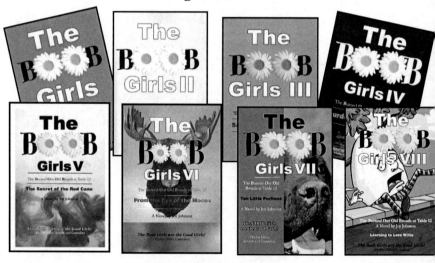

www.theboobgirls.com

Visit the girls and Joy Johnson at:

www.theboobgirls.com

The BOOB Girls are available on Kindle and Nook.

Joy is an international speaker who has presented delightful *Boob Girl* programs across the country.

Ask her about speaking at your group. You can email Joy at joy.johnson@msn.com

Join Joy on Facebook at
Joy Johnson or The BOOB Girls

And sign up for the Girl's blog.
Just email Joy at joy.johnson@msn.com

For information on Joy as a
speaker for your group:
email or call: 402-639-2939